GEORGIAN POETRY

Selected and introduced by
James Reeves

PENGUIN BOOKS

Penguin Books Ltd, Harmondsworth, Middlesex, England
Penguin Books, 625 Madison Avenue, New York, New York 10022, U.S.A.
Penguin Books Australia Ltd, Ringwood, Victoria, Australia
Penguin Books Canada Ltd, 2801 John Street, Markham, Ontario, Canada L3R 1B4
Penguin Books (N.Z.) Ltd, 182–190 Wairau Road, Auckland 10, New Zealand

—

This selection first published 1962
Reprinted 1966, 1968, 1971, 1975, 1981

—

Copyright © James Reeves, 1962
All rights reserved

—

Made and printed in Great Britain
by Richard Clay (The Chaucer Press) Ltd,
Bungay, Suffolk
Set in Monotype Fournier

Contents

Introduction

THE word 'Georgian', as applied to a body of poetry written in English during the second and third decades of the twentieth century, came into use purely as a descriptive term. By the end of that period it had become a term of critical abuse, and by the beginning of the Second World War it was merely an archaism. It might on occasions be employed to describe some belated appearance of a kind of poem now irredeemably discredited; but by 1950 it could no longer be used with the certainty that it would be understood by anyone under twenty-five. 'The Georgians', if the phrase means anything at all to the younger generation of today, is as old-world and remote as 'the nineties'. Yet there was a brief period during which the image of modern poetry in the minds of most educated readers was that presented by the Georgian movement.

The reaction against Georgianism began quietly enough, shortly after the end of the First World War. If dates are needed, it is easy to remember that the word 'Georgian' in our sense was coined in 1912, and that *The Waste Land* was published just ten years later.* But the image of modern poetry presented by Eliot's 'unreal City, under the brown fog of a winter dawn' did not finally replace the earlier one until a decade later. Georgianism continued to enjoy wide popularity at least until the late twenties. The Anglo-American movement which was heralded by the somewhat noisy propaganda of Pound and the theorists of Imagism, and culminated in the triumph of Eliot, took as a starting-point the state to which English poetry was reduced by the efforts of the Georgians. It had the Georgians to react against. Its adherents could use the term 'Georgian' as a term of contempt, and any poet who could claim to be anti-Georgian was sure of a hearing. It was forgotten that, as there might be a bad Imagist, there might also have been a good Georgian. But the Georgians started in reaction against nothing except a general neglect of modern poetry.

* New York, 1922: London, 1923.

The beginnings of the movement were more or less casual
and entirely untheoretical. A bachelor Civil Servant, Edward
Marsh, at that time secretary to Winston Churchill at the Ad-
miralty, was an amateur of the arts. He had no professional con-
nexion with poetry, but he was impressed with the work of cer-
tain of the younger poets, notably Rupert Brooke, who was re-
cently down from Cambridge and about to make a name for
himself in literary circles. The older poets, Bridges, Hardy,
Masefield, and a few others were well established, but there
seemed to be little interest in the work of their juniors. Marsh
and Brooke accordingly conceived the idea of issuing a collec-
tion of modern poems aimed at disturbing public lethargy and
bringing to general attention the existence of a body of unrecog-
nized talent. It was Marsh who invented the title 'Georgian
Poetry', though Brooke considered it somewhat timid and con-
servative. Brooke was something of a rebel, and Marsh was obliged
to soften his friend's rebellious tendencies in order to make the
movement a success. Before the end of 1912 Marsh had gained
the active cooperation of some of the younger poets and the in-
dulgent support of those whose reputations were established.
Harold Monro, editor of *The Poetry Review*, was secured as
publisher, and about the end of the year *Georgian Poetry 1911–
1912* appeared. It contained a brief Prefatory Note declaring
that it was issued 'in the belief that English poetry is now once
again putting on new strength and beauty'. Its aim was to pre-
sent a selection from the most significant new verse then being
published. 'Few readers', Marsh stated, 'have the leisure or zeal
to investigate each volume as it appears.' These emphases were
significant. The great Victorians had died, leaving an aftermath
of ninetyish reaction which did little to stir the interest of the
general public. The great Edwardians were in possession of the
field, but no one was very excited about them. The success of
Masefield's long, colloquial verse narrative, *The Everlasting
Mercy* (1911), which had struck a new note, indicated there was
a wider public prepared to accept new things in poetry, pro-
vided they were made easily available. But this public had not
'the leisure or zeal' to discover the new poets for itself. Marsh

showed himself, therefore, to have a shrewd insight into popular needs when he acted as editor of the new venture. He gave the Georgian movement its essentially *anthological* character. His taste was conservative yet catholic; he did not like experiment; on the other hand, he realized that Victorian stuffiness and didacticism were out of favour. The busy reader, as often as not a professional man or woman with only a week-end interest in the arts, would prefer short, self-contained, lyrical pieces with the accent on 'beauty' rather than 'strength'. They were mistrustful of sordid imagery and shaky syntax; like his readers, Marsh was temperamentally opposed to theories of art and literature. At first Pound was to have been a contributor to the book, but when it became the first of a series, Marsh decided not to include Americans. Accordingly both Pound and Frost, who also was to have contributed, did not appear.

The success of the anthology was immediate, and proved Marsh to have been right in assuming that there was a large public awaiting a particular kind of new poetry, served up in a particular way. He edited no fewer than five volumes between 1912 and 1922, and it is interesting to reflect that, had a sixth volume appeared, Monro, always more in sympathy with modernist and experimental verse, might have persuaded him to include Eliot. But Marsh's instinct in dropping the series in the year of publication of *The Waste Land* was as sound as it had been in starting it ten years earlier. In the five volumes he published work by thirty-six poets, none of whom, with the possible exception of D. H. Lawrence, could have been called modernist. Nor did he entirely cover the field of what can now be seen to have been essentially 'Georgian' poetry. He included a fair proportion of dead wood; and his exclusion both of the older generation, Thomas Hardy for instance, and A. E. Housman, who declined to contribute, as well as most of the experimental writers, confined his choice within somewhat narrow limits. Nevertheless, he achieved his principal aim, which was once more to interest the contemporary reading public in modern poetry. This is often forgotten, but historically it is of importance. The sales of every volume of Georgian poetry were, by

present-day standards, immense; to read and possess Georgian
anthologies, whether the original volumes edited by Marsh or
later ones, became customary among ordinary readers. The
modernists who reacted against the movement thus had a public
to capture. Accordingly, while the Georgians recruited a large
reading public for poetry, the modernist movement, in turning
readers against the Georgians, have to some extent turned them
against poetry. True, a handful of big individual reputations
have been made since the decline of Georgianism; so far as the
general run of contemporary poetry is concerned, however, the
educated public has turned steadily away from it. We may say,
then, that with the Georgians poetry became popular in order to
secure a hearing; with the post-Georgians it became esoteric and
sacrificed its public. Whether this is a good development cannot
be argued here; but in inviting a new generation to re-read the
Georgians, it is necessary to remind them that they are examin-
ing an essentially popular movement.

Marsh was a modest man, but he stuck firmly to his own criti-
cal standards. He believed that they were the standards of a large
educated public, and in this he was right. His outlook, as has
already been suggested, was characteristically English. Theoriz-
ing about art was foreign; announcing aesthetic and critical doc-
trines was foreign. His approach to artistic problems was prag-
matic and amateur. If his formula for an anthology worked, it
was good; if his method succeeded by the light of personal taste,
why adopt rigid critical canons? Marsh was well aware of the
nature of his attitude. Invited to accept the dedication of a new
novel, about 1934, as the figurehead of the Georgian he replied:
'My only slight doubt is whether Georgian poetry isn't too
ancient history to be raked up. I feel towards it now very much as
I should towards having been Captain of Cricket at Westminster.'

The Georgian poets were Marsh's friends; his attitude was
paternal. Brooke and the young poets who accepted his help so
eagerly were his dream-children. As Gosse said in his review of
the fifth and last of the volumes, 'The Georgians ought to be a
happy clan. No other body of writers, since English first began
to be written, has received so much composite attention or has

had its way so comfortably smoothed for it. . . . They have swept along the road together in a comfortable charabanc with E. M. as their beribboned driver.'

Marsh was right to resign his leadership of the clan when he did. It was taken on by J. C. Squire, who proved himself to be entirely sympathetic to the aims of the brotherhood. But long before the demise in 1934 of his literary magazine, *The London Mercury*, he was considered reactionary. Georgianism had for some time been generally regarded as a poetic backwater, the main stream of modern poetry having for some years passed it by. Squire was considered a back number in a way Marsh had never been. The 'Englishness' of the Georgians, in view of the influence of America and Paris on contemporary literature, seemed to stamp them as hopelessly out-of-date and parochial. But this quality had at first commended them. It coincided with popular patriotic sentiment at the time of the First World War. The war gave the movement an almost unforeseen impetus – I say 'almost' because the international scene was already dark when the movement was launched. Marsh combined his work of editing the first volume of *Georgian Poetry* with the greatly in-creased work at the Admiralty consequent upon the expansion of the navy in competition with that of Germany. The celebration of England, whether at peace or at war, became a principal aim of Georgian poetry. The English countryside, English crafts, and English sports offered suitable subject-matter. Poems about country cottages, old furniture, moss-covered barns, rose-scented lanes, apple and cherry orchards, village inns, and vil-lage cricket expressed the nostalgia of the soldier on active ser-vice and the threat to country life which educated readers feared from the growth of urbanism.

Not only was Georgian poetry markedly English and rural in character, its appeal to a wide audience meant that it was un-specialized and easy to understand. A public that had no leisure or zeal to choose its own poetry, but liked it in anthologies, had no time for complicated and obscure themes. The idea that a poem may be easy to understand is something that was killed along with the Georgian movement.

Writing in 1929 Harold Monro, who had a foot in each camp, said that A. E. Housman was the spiritual father of the Georgian movement, while Marsh was its temporal patron. He further correctly diagnosed the position when he added: 'I should say that just as A. E. Housman and Rupert Brooke were very powerful influences up to 1920, so T. S. Eliot will be up to 1940. The former, however, carved jewels, while the latter rough-models out of block granite.'* Housman, in short, was something of a miniaturist, aiming at a limpid clarity of texture, and this was a quality which the Georgians imitated. Moreover Housman's mood of pessimism suited the post-war atmosphere of disillusion. Writing shortly after the war, Graves said: 'With the Armistice and Peace, realistic war-poetry immediately lost its market, and now until the confident poetry of reconstruction can appear in western Europe, the public laurels will be transferred either to civilian poets of scepticism and cynicism, Messrs Hardy and Housman of the elder, Messrs Aldous Huxley and T. S. Eliot of the younger generation, or to the poets of temporary escape, Mr de la Mare, Mr Blunden, the later Masefield, and the middle Yeats.'†

Undoubtedly Hardy was another father-figure to the Georgians: his muse was rustic, he was intensely English, and there was nothing facile about the pessimistic scepticism of his temper.

Under these influences, what Squire called 'an exceptional recent flowering' took place in English poetry in the decade of the First World War. He was writing in 1921, in the preface to his first series of *Selections from Modern Poets*, a somewhat more comprehensive and retrospective anthology than Marsh's volumes. Squire added: 'Should our literary age be remembered by posterity solely as an age during which fifty men had written lyrics of some durability for their truth and beauty, it would not be remembered with contempt. It is in that conviction that I have compiled this anthology.'

Fifty minor poets writing durable lyrics about truth and beauty – that was the image of modern poetry which the Geor-

---

* *Twentieth Century Poetry:* An Anthology. Introduction.
† See *Fashions in Poetry*, reprinted in *The Common Asphodel*.

gian movement projected. No wonder it became discredited in the eyes of discriminating and progressive readers. For the ideal of poetry thus set up demanded no great gifts either of intellect, imagination, or technique. Georgianism attracted not only a number of potentially excellent poets, but also a great many hangers-on, amateurs of truth and beauty, lovers of the English scene who could turn a jewel-like lyric or a light-hearted ballade with the best.

The faults of Georgian poetry at its most ordinary were technical slackness – the use of imprecise diction and facile rhythm; sentimentality of outlook; trivial, and even downright commonplace themes. When certain subjects and attitudes are accepted as intrinsically poetic, it is easy to adopt them, and to go through the motions of writing a poem. One of the ingredients of the standard Georgian anthology recipe was a certain mistrust of rhetoric, of the grand Victorian manner, of grandiose themes. This resulted in a pedestrian tendency which is observable in much run-of-the-mill Georgian poetry – a tendency which too often leads to triviality, complacency, and the avoidance of strong personal feeling. It is possible to jog through volume after volume of Georgian lyrics without being in any way stirred either to applause or to protest. Pleasantness for its own sake is no more moving than unpleasantness. Brooke's 'unforgettable, unforgotten river smell' is no more intrinsically poetic than Eliot's 'smells of steaks in passageways'. Both are significant only as equivalents to certain states of mind. All periods have their recipe poems; those of today are no better and no worse than those of the twenties: only they are more acceptable to contemporary readers.

One of the best of the Georgians, Edmund Blunden, writing at a much later date about a neglected poet of the period, Ivor Gurney, put his finger on some of the weaknesses of Georgian poetry: 'Whatever was attractive and poetically moving to the generation of writers called Georgians was so to him also, and he was content to be of that generation; but neither easy sentiment nor an indifferent "eye on the object" can be imputed to him, nor yet languor nor studied homeliness of expression.'

Easy sentiment, an indifferent eye on the object (imprecise imagery), languor, and studied homeliness of expression – these indeed were some of the ingredients of the Georgian recipe, against which the public stomach was turned in the end. All the qualities which are most admired in the poetry of Eliot and other post-Georgians can be seen as being opposed to these faults. The Georgian movement as a whole was not, as Brooke believed, a movement of rebellion against Victorian romanticism, itself the decadent stage of Wordsworthian romanticism; it was merely the final phase of a long deterioration. Brooke himself revealed a curious complex of influences. His self-conscious 'unpleasantness' and his interest in the Jacobean drama might have made him a modernist had not the romanticism of the early Yeats and the idealistic raptures expected of him held him back. Neither Marsh nor Brooke's older admirers, men like Gosse and Dobson, wholly accepted the 'unpleasant' element in Brooke, whose powers of self-criticism were somewhat blunted by his friend's easy praise. It was Marsh who persuaded him to change the title *The Sentimental Exile* to *The Old Vicarage, Grantchester*; so that what to Brooke was mere facile trifling became one of the stock anthology pieces of the Georgian era. Brooke was somewhat deflected from his purpose as a rebel by premature adulation, and his subsequent canonization entirely obscured the mixed and contradictory character of his real promise and achievement. The real revolt against the romantic tradition came with the anti-Georgian reaction and belongs to the next chapter in literary history.

What then were the positive merits of the poetry which was wholly superseded in critical esteem during the late twenties? What may be salvaged from it? What remains when the dead wood has been thrown on the bonfire? Is there any live growth remaining? For so thoroughly has criticism rejected the Georgian movement, so complete has the revolution been, that these questions have never been answered. The baby had been thrown out with the bath water, and no one has taken the trouble to see whether it perished from neglect or grew up in exile, unregarded but alive.

The present collection is the result of an attempt by one reader to answer these questions. It contains poems by some twenty poets ranging in time from Housman to Andrew Young. It represents a continuous tradition which dates back to the beginning of this century and has continued until about 1950, a tradition which partly ignores, partly rejects, and partly absorbs the modernism represented by Eliot and the poets whose reputations were established in the thirties and later. Something will be said about the interpretation of 'Georgian' here adopted: such a term is always arguable at the periphery, but a glance at the contents of this book will show what I regard as central, about which there can be little disagreement. Among those poets who are central to the Georgian movement at its best were de la Mare, Davies, and the living poet, Edmund Blunden. No one would seriously dispute that the bulk of their work is Georgian in character: their best poems are Georgian poems. The same may be said of Siegfried Sassoon, who also belongs to a group whose most significant work was inspired by the First World War – Owen and Edward Thomas being chief among the others. Brooke also must be classed as a war poet, but his best work, in my opinion, belongs to the period before 1914. Graves too was a full member of the Georgian brotherhood so far as the war period is concerned. His most significant work, which is not represented here, has, however, been done since the decline of Georgianism. It cannot be called Georgian. Had Wilfred Owen lived, it is certain that he would have had to appear as an ex-Georgian. It is significant that of the poets represented in these pages, only Owen and Graves appeared in Michael Roberts' *Faber Book of Modern Verse* (1935). This indicates the completeness of the break between the Georgian tradition and what was considered 'modern' in the thirties. Now that that revolution has, so to speak, settled down and become a historical fact rather than a matter of contention, it is possible to take a new look at the earlier tradition and see whether anything produced by it ought to be regarded as 'modern' – that is, as having a claim on the attention of contemporary readers.

When I say that I have chosen the poems in this book for

what is to me their 'permanent' value – or to put it in another way, their 'modernity' – I do not presume to judge of the Georgians *sub specie aeternitatis*. I mean simply that they are worthy of the attention of the contemporary reader. I would go further and say that to reject these poems and allow the titles of 'modernity' or 'significance' only to post-Georgian poetry, is to deprive ourselves of something valuable; it is to convict ourselves of a limited, and even distorted view of poetry. The Georgians can offer virtues which seem to have deserted modern poetry and which might be regained if we want to see poetry once more in its wholeness. These qualities are: natural simplicity, emotional warmth, and moral innocence. When I mentioned Davies recently to a literary critic and historian, he said, 'Davies? Oh, he was a sort of natural, wasn't he – like Clare?' The critical fashion which places complexity as the highest of the poetic virtues is in danger of taking an unjustifiably one-sided view. Any view of poetry which can find no place for Clare or Davies is surely limited. It is impossible to contemplate the life and work of either of these poets without being aware of their wholly poetic character: both wrote too much, and their complete poems contain a great deal that is slack, flat, or repetitive. But at their best they have a warmth of feeling, a directness of response, and a naturalness of utterance which place them beyond mere fashion. They are not to be dismissed merely because their emotions are uncomplicated. If any reader, anxious for technical novelty, looks at the poems of Davies and says, 'Yes, but it has been done before,' I can only answer, 'Read *Hospital Waiting Room* or *The Tugged Hand*, and tell me by whom.' To be new, a feeling does not necessarily demand radical novelty of expression.

Warmth of emotion is observable also in poems by Graves, Sassoon, Blunden, and de la Mare. Each has a personal contribution to make in response to a given private or public situation. Where they are most clearly differentiated from the post-Georgians is in their accessibility to unsophisticated emotion. It is this sophistication, pre-eminent in the early poems of Eliot, which is lacking in the Georgians; lack of sophistication is perhaps the principal barrier between the modern reader and the Georgians. To read almost any poetry since 1935 which is currently considered significant is to be aware of this sophistication: it reveals itself mainly in a mistrust of direct emotion, of a simple response to primary experience, and of direct passionate utterance. The most characteristic poetry of today expresses anxiety, self-doubt, and self-hate, a sense of knowing too much, fear of being caught with the heart exposed. It is technically irreproachable – which, at its worst, means that it is well able to conceal poverty of content behind abundant verbal resource. It looks back to the early Eliot, whose atmosphere is charged with an oppressive sense of guilt. The modern poet is obliged to be tortured. If he is not, he is suspect. There are good modern poets who are untortured – e. e. cummings, for instance – but they are always open to suspicion. The comparative innocence of the Georgians, then, is another stumbling-block to their re-admission. But there may be virtue in innocence, as in guilt.

These are some of the factors which have guided me in making this selection. I do not claim to have looked at the Georgians with any eye but that of 1960. If, to revert to Marsh's original declaration, I have chosen to illustrate their 'strength' rather than their 'beauty', it is because the former seems to me to have more immediate appeal. The 'beauty' of Georgian poetry has been amply illustrated in the many anthologies of the twenties. I have tried to avoid the idea of a chorus of fifty talented songsters, and have aimed at giving a more solid view of the principal Georgians than was possible in those earlier selections. I have avoided most of the stock anthology pieces, since their endless repetition tended to distort the reputations of their authors. Davies believed *The Kingfisher* was his best poem; that was typical of him. He knew that its pretentious diction and spurious simplicity would recommend it to the amateur of anthologies.

My determining object has been to make a selection of Georgian poetry which will appeal to the unprejudiced modern reader after a generation of neglect. In order to do this, I have had to avoid two courses open to me. First, it seemed wrong to attempt a historical retrospect of the whole Georgian movement – to present the Georgians as they would have appeared to themselves in the year 1920 or thereabouts. That has been done by Squire and others. As a highly popular movement, it attracted to itself two classes of poets whom this selection has nothing to do with: on the one hand, what might be called the 'regulars' – those who turned up in every volume of Marsh's series and who produced periodical slim volumes of 'recipe' poems which once enjoyed a wide circulation but now seem to be altogether lacking in appeal. On the other hand, there were the occasional contributors, who could be relied on to turn out the odd lyric or two which found their way into all the anthologies. Perhaps there will be a time when a full-sized historical conspectus of the Georgians is called for, in which every poet once thought important will find his due place. That time has not yet arrived. Nevertheless, I am sure that many readers who are sympathetic to my general purpose, especially among the older generation, will condemn the omission of certain poets. I can only say that I have given them all a fair hearing. I have no confidence in my ability to recommend all the old favourites of my older friends. I would prefer my younger readers to say, 'So this is what we have missed' – not, 'So this is what they used to read.'

A more insidious temptation was to improve my selection by including poems which are not properly Georgian, even though they were written in the period under review. But I felt bound to play fair with the reader. He does not need to be told that Hardy was a great lyric poet or that Yeats wrote some of his most admired pieces in the Georgian period. Hardy and Yeats were not Georgians, though their influence was strong. Some may query my inclusion of Housman on chronological grounds; I have accordingly included only poems from his 1922 volume. The Poet Laureate may seem inadequately represented, but to me his best work is contained in poems too long to include; and I could not get his permission to reprint what seems to me the best of his shorter pieces. It was more tempting to include D. H. Lawrence, who appeared – incongruously, I cannot help thinking – in all but one of Marsh's volumes. But Lawrence was not a

Georgian in any real sense, and I could not feel justified in admitting him.

The list of possible inclusions might be continued almost indefinitely. Every reader familiar with the poetry of the Georgian period could question some of my exclusions as well as my inclusions. This is a personal selection, but I hope it is not wilfully so. I hope that my juniors will read these poems for their own sake, and that my elders will forgive any apparent idiosyncrasy of judgement. I was an undergraduate at the very moment in literary history when the Georgian image of modern poetry was being replaced – rather ostentatiously in some quarters – by the later one. I attended the funeral. To attempt a reappraisal of the Georgians is rather like doing belated justice to the memory of one's father. There is an irreverent popular song which begins

> Father's picture's hanging in the hall
> Next to the picture of the monkey on the wall.

It now seems to me wrong to have made a monkey out of my poetic father. But I believe that a new evolution of literary taste makes it possible once more to appreciate him 'in his habit as he lived'.

J.R.

Chalfont St Giles
1960

Acknowledgements

Permission to use copyright material is gratefully acknowledged to the following:

Mr Edmund Blunden for poems by him; Messrs Sidgwick and Jackson Ltd and Messrs McClelland and Stewart Ltd of Toronto for poems by Rupert Brooke. Mrs H. M. Davies and Messrs Jonathan Cape Ltd for poems from *Collected Poems* by W. H. Davies; the Literary Trustees of Walter de la Mare and the Society of Authors for poems by Walter de la Mare; Messrs J. M. Dent & Sons Ltd for poems by James Elroy Flecker; the Hutchinson Group for poems from *Collected Poems* (1954) by Ivor Gurney; Mr Robert Graves for poems from *Collected Poems* 1959 (Cassell) and other volumes; Mr Ralph Hodgson and Messrs Macmillan & Co. Ltd for a poem from *Poems*; the Society of Authors, the Trustees of the author's Estate, and Messrs Jonathan Cape Ltd for poems from *Collected Poems* by A. E. Housman; Dr John Masefield o.m., the Society of Authors, and the Macmillan Co. of New York for poems by John Masefield; Mrs Alida Monro and Messrs Gerald Duckworth & Co. Ltd for a poem by Harold Monro; Mr Harold Owen and Messrs Chatto & Windus Ltd for poems by Wilfred Owen; The Hon. Victoria Sackville-West for a poem by her. Mr Siegfried Sassoon for poems by him; the Syndics of the Cambridge University Press for poems by Charles Sorley; Mr Raglan Squire and Messrs Macmillan & Co. Ltd for a poem from the *Collected Poems of Sir John Squire*; Mrs Stephens and Messrs Macmillan & Co. Ltd for poems from *Collected Poems* by James Stephens; Mrs Helen Thomas for poems by Edward Thomas; Messrs Rupert Hart-Davis Ltd for poems by Andrew Young.

Among critical and other works consulted, the Editor wishes especially to acknowledge his indebtedness to Christopher Hassall's invaluable *Edward Marsh: A Biography* (Longmans, 1959).

Alfred Edward Housman

'Her strong enchantments failing'

Her strong enchantments failing,
    Her towers of fear in wreck,
Her limbecks dried of poisons
    And the knife at her neck,

The Queen of air and darkness
    Begins to shrill and cry,
'O young man, O my slayer,
    Tomorrow you shall die.'

O Queen of air and darkness,
    I think 'tis truth you say,
And I shall die tomorrow;
    But you will die today.

'In valleys green and still'

In valleys green and still
    Where lovers wander maying
They hear from over the hill
    A music playing.

Behind the drum and fife,
    Past hawthornwood and hollow,
Through earth and out of life
    The soldiers follow.

The soldier's is the trade:
    In any wind or weather
He steals the heart of maid
    And man together.

The lover and his lass
    Beneath the hawthorn lying
Have heard the soldiers pass,
    And both are sighing.

And down the distance they
    With dying note and swelling
Walk the resounding way
    To the still dwelling.

'The laws of God, the laws of man'

The laws of God, the laws of man,
He may keep that will and can;
Not I: let God and man decree
Laws for themselves and not for me;
And if my ways are not as theirs
Let them mind their own affairs.
Their deeds I judge and much condemn,
Yet when did I make laws for them?
Please yourselves, say I, and they
Need only look the other way.
But no, they will not; they must still
Wrest their neighbour to their will,
And make me dance as they desire
With jail and gallows and hell-fire.
And how am I to face the odds
Of man's bedevilment and God's?
I, a stranger and afraid
In a world I never made.

They will be master, right or wrong;
Though both are foolish, both are strong.
And since, my soul, we cannot fly
To Saturn nor to Mercury,
Keep we must, if keep we can,
These foreign laws of God and man.

The Culprit

The night my father got me
  His mind was not on me;
He did not plague his fancy
  To muse if I should be
  The son you see.

The day my mother bore me
  She was a fool and glad,
For all the pain I cost her
  That she had borne the lad
  That born she had.

My mother and my father
  Out of the light they lie;
The warrant would not find them,
  And here 'tis only I
  Shall hang so high.

Oh let not man remember
  The soul that God forgot,
But fetch the county kerchief
  And noose me in the knot,
  And I will rot.

For so the game is ended
   That should not have begun.
My father and my mother
   They had a likely son,
   And I have none.

'*Tell me not here, it needs not saying*'

Tell me not here, it needs not saying,
   What tune the enchantress plays
In aftermaths of soft September
   Or under blanching mays,
For she and I were long acquainted
   And I knew all her ways.

On russet floors, by waters idle,
   The pine lets fall its cone;
The cuckoo shouts all day at nothing
   In leafy dells alone;
And traveller's joy beguiles in autumn
   Hearts that have lost their own.

On acres of the seeded grasses
   The changing burnish heaves;
Or marshalled under moons of harvest
   Stand still all night the sheaves;
Or beeches strip in storms for winter
   And stain the wind with leaves.

Possess, as I possessed a season,
   The countries I resign,
Where over elmy plains the highway
   Would mount the hills and shine,
And full of shade the pillared forest
   Would murmur and be mine.

For nature, heartless, witless nature,
  Will neither care nor know
What stranger's feet may find the meadow
  And trespass there and go,
Nor ask amid the dews of morning
  If they are mine or no.

W. H. Davies

A Dream

I met her in the leafy woods,
  Early a Summer's night;
I saw her white teeth in the dark,
  There was no better light.

Had she not come up close and made
  Those lilies their light spread,
I had not proved her mouth a rose,
  So round, so fresh, so red.

Her voice was gentle, soft and sweet,
  In words she was not strong;
Yet her low twitter had more charm
  Than any full-mouthed song.

We walked in silence to her cave,
  With but few words to say;
But ever and anon she stopped
  For kisses on the way.

And after every burning kiss
  She laughed and danced around;
Back-bending, with her breasts straight up,
  Her hair it touched the ground.

When we lay down, she held me fast,
  She held me like a leech;
Ho, ho! I know what her red tongue
  Is made for, if not speech.

And what is this, how strange, how sweet!
  Her teeth are made to bite
The man she gives her passion to,
  And not to boast their white.

O night of Joy! O morning's grief!
  For when, with passion done,
Rocked on her breast I fell asleep,
  I woke, and lay alone.

Sweet Stay-at-Home

Sweet Stay-at-Home, sweet Well-content,
Thou knowest of no strange continent:
Thou hast not felt thy bosom keep
A gentle motion with the deep;
Thou hast not sailed in Indian seas,
Where scent comes forth in every breeze.
Thou hast not seen the rich grape grow
For miles, as far as eyes can go;
Thou hast not seen a summer's night
When maids could sew by a worm's light;
Nor the North Sea in spring send out
Bright hues that like birds flit about
In solid cages of white ice –
Sweet Stay-at-Home, sweet Love-one-place.
Thou hast not seen black fingers pick
White cotton when the bloom is thick,
Nor heard black throats in harmony;
Nor hast thou sat on stones that lie
Flat on the earth, that once did rise
To hide proud kings from common eyes;
Thou hast not seen plains full of bloom
Where green things had such little room

They pleased the eye like fairer flowers –
Sweet Stay-at-Home, all these long hours.
Sweet Well-content, sweet Love-one-place,
Sweet, simple maid, bless thy dear face;
For thou hast made more homely stuff
Nurture thy gentle self enough;
I love thee for a heart that's kind –
Not for the knowledge in thy mind.

Heaven

That paradise the Arab dreams,
Is far less sand and more fresh streams.
The only heaven an Indian knows,
Is hunting deer and buffaloes.
The Yankee heaven – to bring Fame forth
By some freak show of what he's worth.
The heaven that fills an English heart,
Is Union Jacks in every part.
The Irish heaven is heaven of old,
When Satan cracked skulls manifold.
The Scotsman has his heaven to come –
To argue his Creator dumb.
The Welshman's heaven is singing airs –
No matter who feels sick and swears.

The Hospital Waiting-Room

We wait our turn, as still as mice,
For medicine free, and free advice:
Two mothers, and their little girls
So small – each one with flaxen curls –
And I myself, the last to come.
Now as I entered that bare room,
I was not seen or heard; for both
The mothers – one in finest cloth,
With velvet blouse and crocheted lace,
Lips painted red, and powdered face;
The other ragged, whose face took
Its own dull, white, and wormy look –
Exchanged a hard and bitter stare.
And both the children, sitting there,
Taking example from that sight,
Made ugly faces, full of spite.
This woman said, though not a word
From her red painted lips was heard –
'Why have I come to this, to be
In such a slattern's company?'
The ragged woman's look replied –
'If you can dress with so much pride,
Why are you here, so neat and nice,
For medicine free, and free advice?'
And I, who needed richer food,
Not medicine, to help my blood;
Who could have swallowed then a horse,
And chased its rider round the course,
Sat looking on, ashamed, perplexed,
Until a welcome voice cried – 'Next!'

The Inquest

I took my oath I would inquire,
 Without affection, hate, or wrath,
Into the death of Ada Wright –
 So help me God! I took that oath.

When I went out to see the corpse,
 The four months' babe that died so young,
I judged it was seven pounds in weight,
 And little more than one foot long.

One eye, that had a yellow lid,
 Was shut – so was the mouth, that smiled;
The left eye open, shining bright –
 It seemed a knowing little child.

For as I looked at that one eye,
 It seemed to laugh, and say with glee:
'What caused my death you'll never know –
 Perhaps my mother murdered me.'

When I went into court again,
 To hear the mother's evidence –
It was a love-child, she explained.
 And smiled, for our intelligence.

'Now, Gentlemen of the Jury,' said
 The coroner – 'this woman's child
By misadventure met its death.'
 'Aye, aye,' said we. The mother smiled.

And I could see that child's one eye
 Which seemed to laugh, and say with glee:
'What caused my death you'll never know –
 Perhaps my mother murdered me.'

The Two Children

'Ah, little boy! I see
    You have a wooden spade.
Into this sand you dig
    So deep – for what?' I said.
'There's more rich gold,' said he,
    'Down under where I stand,
Than twenty elephants
    Could move across the land.'

'Ah, little girl with wool! –
    What are you making now?'
'Some stockings for a bird,
    To keep his legs from snow.'
And there those children are,
    So happy, small, and proud:
The boy that digs his grave,
    The girl that knits her shroud.

The Power of Silence

And will she never hold her tongue,
    About that feather in her hat;
    Her scarf, when she has done with that,
And then the bangle on her wrist,
    And is my silence meant to make
Her talk the more – the more she's kissed?

At last, with silence matching mine,
    She feels the passion deep and strong,
    That fears to trust a timid tongue.
Say, Love – that draws us close together –
    Isn't she the very life of Death?
No more of bangle, scarf or feather.

Confession

One hour in every hundred hours
I sing of childhood, birds and flowers;
Who reads my character in song
Will not see much in me that's wrong.

But in my ninety hours and nine
I would not tell what thoughts are mine:
They're not so pure as find their words
In songs of childhood, flowers and birds.

My Old Acquaintance

Working her toothless gums till her sharp chin
Could almost reach and touch her sharper nose,
These are the words my old acquaintance said:
'I have four children, all alive and well;
My eldest girl was seventy years in March,
And though when she was born her body was
Covered all over with black hair, and long
Which when I saw at first made me cry out,
'Take it away, it is a monkey – ugh!'
Yet she's as smooth and fair as any, now.
And I, who sit for hours in this green space
That has seven currents of good air, and pray
At night to Jesus and his Mother, live
In hopes to reach my ninetieth year in June.
But ere it pleases God to take my soul,
I'll sell my fine false teeth, which cost five pounds,
Preserved in water now for twenty years,
For well I know those girls will fight for them
As soon as I am near my death; before
My skin's too cold to feel the feet of flies.

God bless you and good day – I wish you well.
For me, I cannot relish food, or sleep
Till God sees fit to hold the Kaiser fast,
Stabbed, shot, or hanged – and his black soul
Sent into hell, to bubble, burn and squeal;
Think of the price of fish – and look at bacon!'

I am the Poet Davies, William

I am the Poet Davies, William,
   I sin without a blush or blink:
I am a man that lives to eat;
   I am a man that lives to drink.

My face is large, my lips are thick,
   My skin is coarse and black almost;
But the ugliest feature is my verse,
   Which proves my soul is black and lost.

Thank heaven thou didst not marry me,
   A poet full of blackest evil;
For how to manage my damned soul
   Will puzzle many a flaming devil.

The Villain

While joy gave clouds the light of stars,
   That beamed where'er they looked;
And calves and lambs had tottering knees,
   Excited, while they sucked;
While every bird enjoyed his song,
Without one thought of harm or wrong –

I turned my head and saw the wind,
   Not far from where I stood,
Dragging the corn by her golden hair,
   Into a dark and lonely wood.

One Thing Wanting

'Your life was hard with mangling clothes,
   You scrubbed our floors for years;
   But now, your children are so good,
   That you can rest your poor old limbs,
   And want for neither drink nor meat.'
'It's true,' she said, and laughed for joy;
   And still her voice, with all her years,
   Could make a song-bird wonder if
   A rival sweetness challenged him.
   But soon her face was full of trouble:
'If only I could tear,' she said,
'My sister Alice out of her grave –
   Who taunted me when I was poor –
   And make her understand these words:
"See, I have everything I want,
   My children, Alice, are so good" –
   If I could only once do that,
   There's nothing else I want on earth.'

Beggar's Song

Good people keep their holy day,
   They rest from labour on a Sunday;
But we keep holy every day,
   And rest from Monday until Monday.

And yet the noblest work on earth
  Is done when beggars do their part:
They work, dear ladies, on the soft
  And tender feelings in your heart.

A Child's Fancy

His chin went up and down, and chewed at nothing,
His back was bent – the man was old and tired;
Toothless and frail, he hobbled on his way,
Admiring nothing and by none admired;
Unless it was that child, with eager eyes,
Who stared amazed to see so strange a man,
And hobbled home himself, with shoulders raised
Trying to make his chin go up and down;
Unless it was that much affected child,
With rounded shoulders, like the old man seen –
Who asked his mother why he was not made
The wonderful strange sight he might have been.

Love Lights his Fire

Love lights his fire to burn my Past –
  There goes the house where I was born!
And even Friendship – Love declares –
  Must feed his precious flames and burn.

I stuffed my life with odds and ends,
  But how much joy can Knowledge give?
The World my guide, I lived to learn –
  From Love, alone, I learn to live.

Competitors

I had a friend to smoke and drink,
  We dined at clubs and saw the Play;
Till Love came, like the smallest wind,
  And looked him quietly away.

So Friendship goes, and Love remains,
  And who can question which is best —
A Friendship reared on the bottle, or
  A Love that's reared at the breast?

The Ghost

Seek not to know Love's full extent,
  For Death, not Life, must measure Love;
Not till one lover's dead and gone,
  Is Love made strong enough to prove.
What woman, with a ghostly lover,
  Can hold a mirror to her hair?
A man can tell his love with tears,
  When but a woman's ghost is there.
Our greatest meeting is to come,
  When either you or I are lost:
When one, being left alone in tears,
  Confesses to the other's ghost.

Beauty and Brain

When I was old, and she was young,
    With all the beauty hers –
I wooed her with a silver tongue,
    With music for her ears;
And shall I now complain to find
That Beauty has so small a mind?

If this young Chit had had more sense
    Would she have married me?
That she gave me the preference,
    Proved what a fool was she:
Then let me die if I complain
That Beauty has too small a brain.

The Faithful One

The bird that fills my ears with song,
    The Sun that warms me with his fire;
The dog that licks my face and hands,
    And She whose beauty I desire –
Each of these think that he or she
Creates in me the joy they see.

But when my dog's gone off with a bitch,
    And there's no Sun, nor bird in song;
When Love's false eyes seek other men,
    And leave me but her lying tongue;
Still will my Joy – though forced to roam –
Remember me and come back home.

The Birth of Song

I am as certain of my song,
  When first it warms my brain,
As woman of her unborn child,
  Or wind that carries rain.
The child and rain are born at last,
  Though now concealed from sight –
So let my song, unshaped and crude,
  Come perfect to the light.

The Tugged Hand

I have no ears or eyes
  For either bird or flower;
Music and lovely blooms
  Must bide their lighter hour;
So let them wait awhile –
  For yet another day

Till I at last forget
  The woman lying dead;
And how a lonely child
  Came to his mother's bed
And tugged at her cold hand –
  And could not make it play.

All in June

A week ago I had a fire,
    To warm my feet, my hands and face;
Cold winds, that never make a friend,
    Crept in and out of every place.

Today, the fields are rich in grass,
    And buttercups in thousands grow;
I'll show the World where I have been –
    With gold-dust seen on either shoe.

Till to my garden back I come,
    Where bumble-bees, for hours and hours,
Sit on their soft, fat, velvet bums,
    To wriggle out of hollow flowers.

Ralph Hodgson

Eve

Eve, with her basket, was
Deep in the bells and grass,
Wading in bells and grass
Up to her knees,
Picking a dish of sweet
Berries and plums to eat,
Down in the bells and grass
Under the trees.

Mute as a mouse in a
Corner the cobra lay,
Curled round a bough of the
Cinnamon tall ...
Now to get even and
Humble proud heaven and
Now was the moment or
Never at all.

'Eva!' Each syllable
Light as a flower fell,
'Eva!' he whispered the
Wondering maid,
Soft as a bubble sung
Out of a linnet's lung,
Soft and most silverly
'Eva!' he said.

Picture that orchard sprite,
Eve, with her body white,

Supple and smooth to her
Slim finger tips,
Wondering, listening,
Eve with a berry
Half-way to her lips.

Oh had our simple Eve
Seen through the make-believe!
Had she but known the
Pretender he was!
Out of the boughs he came
Whispering still her name
Tumbling in twenty rings
Into the grass.

Here was the strangest pair
In the world anywhere;
Eve in the bells and grass
Kneeling, and he
Telling his story low ...
Singing birds saw them go
Down the dark path to
The Blasphemous Tree.

Oh what a clatter when
Titmouse and Jenny Wren
Saw him successful and
Taking his leave!
How the birds rated him,
How they all hated him!
How they all pitied
Poor motherless Eve!

Picture her crying
Outside in the lane,
Eve, with no dish of sweet
Berries and plums to eat,

Haunting the gate of the
Orchard in vain ...
Picture the lewd delight
Under the hill tonight –
'Eva!' the toast goes round,
'Eva!' again.

Walter de la Mare

Sea-Magic

To R.I.

My heart faints in me for the distant sea.
   The roar of London is the roar of ire
   The lion utters in his old desire
For Libya out of dim captivity.

The long bright silver of Cheapside I see,
   Her gilded weathercocks on roof and spire
   Exulting eastward in the western fire;
All things recall one heart-sick memory: –

Ever the rustle of the advancing foam,
   The surges' desolate thunder, and the cry
   As of some lone babe in the whispering sky;
Ever I peer into the restless gloom
   To where a ship clad dim and loftily
Looms steadfast in the wonder of her home.

Drugged

Inert in his chair,
In a candle's guttering glow;
His bottle empty,
His fire sunk low;
With drug-sealed lids shut fast,
Unsated mouth ajar,
This darkened phantasm walks
Where nightmares are:

51

In a frenzy of life and light,
Crisscross – a menacing throng –
They gibe, they squeal at the stranger,
Jostling along,
Their faces cadaverous grey:
While on high from an attic stare
Horrors, in beauty apparelled,
Down the dark air.

A stream gurgles over its stones,
The chambers within are afire.
Stumble his shadowy feet
Through shine, through mire;
And the flames leap higher.
In vain yelps the wainscot mouse;
In vain beats the hour;
Vacant, his body must drowse
Until daybreak flower –

Staining these walls with its rose,
And the draughts of the morning shall stir
Cold on cold brow, cold hands.
And the wanderer
Back to flesh house must return.
Lone soul – in horror to see,
Than dream more meagre and awful,
Reality.

The Feckless Dinner Party

'Who are we waiting for?' '*Soup* burnt?' ... Eight –
  'Only the tiniest party. – Us!'
'Darling! Divine!' 'Ten minutes late –'
  'And my digest—' 'I'm *ra*venous!'

' "Toomes"?' – 'Oh, he's new.' 'Looks crazed, I guess.'
  ' "Married" – *Again!*' 'Well; more or less!'

'Dinner is *served*!' ' "Dinner is served"!'
  'Is served?' 'Is served.' 'Ah, yes.'

'Dear Mr Prout, will you take down
  The Lilith in leaf-green by the fire?
Blanche Ogleton? ...' 'How coy a frown! –
  Hasn't she borrowed *Eve*'s attire?'
'Morose Old Adam!' 'Charmed – I vow.'
  'Come then, and meet her now.'

'Now, Dr Mallus – would you please? –
  Our daring poetess, Delia Seek?'
'The lady with the bony knees?'
  'And – *entre nous* – less song than beak.'
'Sharing her past with Simple Si—'
  '*Bare* facts! He'll blush!' 'Oh, fie!'

'And *you*, Sir Nathan – false but fair! –
  That fountain of wit, Aurora Pert.'
'More wit than It, poor dear! But there ...'
  'Pitiless Pasha! *And* such a flirt!'
' "Flirt"! *Me?*' 'Who else?' 'You here. ... Who can ...?'
  'In*cor*rigible man!'

'And now, Mr Simon – Little me! –
  Last and –' 'By no means least!' 'Oh, come!
What naughty, naughty flattery!
  Honey! – I *hear* the creature hum!'
'Sweets for the sweet, *I* always say!'
  ' "Always"? ... We're last.' '*This* way?' ...

'No, sir; straight on, please.' 'I'd have vowed! –
   I came the other ...' 'It's queer; I'm sure ...'
'What frightful pictures!' 'Fiends!' 'The *crowd*!'
   'Such news!' 'I can't endure ...'

'Yes, *there* they go.' 'Heavens! *Are* we right!'
   'Follow up closer!' ' "Prout"? – sand-blind!'
'This endless ...' 'Who's turned down the light?'
   'Keep calm! They're close behind.'

'Oh! Dr Mallus; what dismal stairs!'
   'I hate these old Victor ...' 'Dry rot!'
'Darker and darker!' 'Fog!' 'The air's ...'
   'Scarce breathable!' 'Hell!' '*What?*'

'The banister's gone!' 'It's deep; keep close!'
   'We're going down and down!' 'What fun!'
'Damp! Why, my shoes ...' 'It's slimy .... Not *moss*!'
   'I'm freezing cold!' 'Let's run.'

'... Behind us. I'm giddy. ...' 'The catacombs ...'
   'That shout!' 'Who's there?' 'I'm *alone*!' 'Stand back!'
'She said, Lead ...' 'Oh!' 'Where's Toomes?' '*Toomes!*'
   'TOOMES!'
   'Stifling!' 'My skull will crack!'

'Sir Nathan! *Ai!*' 'I *say*! *Toomes!* Prout!'
   'Where? Where?' ' "Our silks and fine array" ...'
'She's mad.' 'I'm dying!' 'Oh, let me *out*!'
   'My God! We've lost our way!' ...

And now how sad-serene the abandoned house,
Whereon at dawn the spring-tide sunbeams beat;
And time's slow pace alone is ominous,
And naught but shadows of noonday therein meet;
Domestic microcosm, only a Trump could rouse:
And, pondering darkly, in the silent rooms,
He who misled them all – the butler, Toomes.

'Dry August Burned'

Dry August burned. A harvest hare
Limp on the kitchen table lay,
Its fur blood-blubbered, eyes astare,
While a small child that stood near by
Wept out her heart to see it there.

Sharp came the *clop* of hoofs, the clang
Of dangling chain, voices that rang.
Out like a leveret she ran,
To feast her glistening bird-clear eyes
On a team of field artillery,
Gay, to manoeuvres, thudding by.
Spur and gun and limber plate
Flashed in the sun. Alert, elate,
Noble horses, foam at lip,
Harness, stirrup, holster, whip,
She watched the sun-tanned soldiery,
Till dust-white hedge had hidden away –
Its din into a rumour thinned –
The laughing, jolting, wild array:
And then – the wonder and tumult gone –
Stood nibbling a green leaf, alone,
Her dark eyes, dreaming. ... She turned, and ran,
Elf-like, in to the house again.
The hare had vanished. ... 'Mother,' she said,
Her tear-stained cheek now flushed with red,
'Please, may I go and see it skinned?'

The Marionettes

Let the foul Scene proceed:
    There's laughter in the wings;
'Tis sawdust that they bleed,
    Only a box Death brings.

How rare a skill is theirs —
    These extreme pangs to show,
How real a frenzy wears
    Each feigner of woe!

Gigantic dins uprise!
    Even the gods must feel
A smarting of the eyes
    As these fumes upsweel.

Strange, such a Piece is free,
    While we Spectators sit,
Aghast at its agony,
    Yet absorbed in it!

Dark is the outer air,
    Coldly the night draughts blow,
Mutely we stare, and stare
    At the frenzied Show.

Yet heaven hath its quiet shroud
    Of deep, immutable blue —
We cry 'An end!' We are bowed
    By the dread, 'It's true!'

While the Shape who hoots applause
    Behind our deafened ear,
Hoots — angel-wise — 'the Cause!'
    And affrights even fear.

Good Company

The stranger from the noisy inn
Strode out into the quiet night,
Tired of the slow sea-faring men.

The wind blew fitfully in his face;
He smelt the salt, and tasted it,
In that sea-haunted, sandy place.

Dim ran the road down to the sea
Bowered in with trees, and solitary;
Ever the painted sign swang slow –
An Admiral staring moodily.

The stranger heard its silly groan;
The beer-mugs rattling to and fro;
The drawling gossip: and the glow
Streamed thro' the door on weed and stone.

Better this star-sown solitude,
The empty night-road to the sea,
Than company so dull and rude.

He smelt the nettles sour and lush,
About him went the bat's shrill cry,
Pale loomed the fragrant hawthorn-bush.

And all along the sunken road –
Green with its weeds, though sandy dry –
Bugloss, hemlock and succory –
The night-breeze wavered from the sea.
And soon upon the beach he stood.

A myriad pebbles in the faint
Horned radiance of a sinking moon
Shone like the rosary of a saint –

A myriad pebbles which, through time,
The bitter tides had visited,
Flood and ebb, by a far moon led,
Noon and night and morning-prime.

He stood and eyed the leaping sea,
The long grey billows surging on,
Baying in sullen unison
Their dirge of agelong mystery.

And, still morose, he went his way,
Over the mounded shingle strode,
And reached a shimmering sand that lay
Where transient bubbles of the froth
Like eyes upon the moonshine glowed,
Faint-coloured as the evening moth.

But not on these the stranger stared,
Nor on the stars that spanned the deep,
But on a body, flung at ease,
As if upon the shore asleep,
Hushed by the rocking seas.

Of a sudden the air was wild with cries —
Shrill and high and violent,
Fled fast a soot-black cormorant,
'Twixt ocean and the skies.

It seemed the sea was like a heart
That stormily a secret keeps
Of what it dare to none impart.
And all its waves rose, heaped and high —
And communed with the moon-grey sky.

The stranger eyed the sailor there,
Mute, and stark, and sinister —
His stiffening sea-clothes grey with salt;
His matted hair, his eyes ajar,
And glazed after the three-fold fear.

And ever the billows cried again
Over the rounded pebble stones,
Baying that heedless sailor-man.

He frowned and glanced up into the air –
Where star with star all faintly shone,
Cancer and the Scorpion,
In ancient symbol circling there:

Gazed inland over the vacant moor;
But ancient silence, and a wind
That whirls upon a sandy floor,
Were now its sole inhabitants.

Forthwith, he wheeled about – away
From the deep night's sad radiance;
The yells of gulls and cormorants
Rang shrilly in his mind.

Pursued by one who noiseless trod,
Whose sharp scythe whistled as he went,
O'er sand and shingle, tuft and sod,
Like hunted hare he coursing ran,
Nor stayed until he came again
Back to the old convivial inn –
The mugs, the smoke, the muffled din –
Packed with its slow-tongued sailor-men.

Rose

Three centuries now are gone
Since Thomas Campion
Left me his airs, his verse, his heedful prose.
Few other memories
Have we of him, or his
And, of his sister, none, but that her name was Rose.

Woodruff, far moschatel
May the more fragrant smell
When into brittle dust their blossoming goes.
His, too, a garden sweet,
Where rarest beauties meet,
And, as a child, he shared them with this Rose.

Faded, past changing, now,
Cheek, mouth, and childish brow.
Where, too, her phantom wanders no man knows.
Yet, when in undertone
That eager lute pines on,
Pleading of things he loved, it sings of Rose.

All That's Past

Very old are the woods;
  And the buds that break
Out of the brier's boughs,
  When March winds wake,
So old with their beauty are —
  Oh, no man knows
Through what wild centuries
  Roves back the rose.

Very old are the brooks;
   And the rills that rise
Where snow sleeps cold beneath
   The azure skies
Sing such a history
   Of come and gone,
Their every drop is as wise
   As Solomon.

Very old are we men;
   Our dreams are tales
Told in dim Eden
   By Eve's nightingales;
We wake and whisper awhile,
   But, the day gone by,
Silence and sleep like fields
   Of amaranth lie.

Echo

'Who called?' I said, and the words
   Through the whispering glades,
Hither, thither, baffled the birds –
   'Who called? Who called?'

The leafy boughs on high
   Hissed in the sun;
The dark air carried my cry
   Faintingly on:

Eyes in the green, in the shade,
   In the motionless brake,
Voices that said what I said,
   For mockery's sake:

'Who cares?' I bawled through my tears;
  The wind fell low:
In the silence, 'Who cares? Who cares?'
  Wailed to and fro.

In a Library

Would – would that there were
A book on that shelf
To teach an old man
To teach himself! –

The joy of some scribe,
Brush in service to quill,
Who, with bird, flower, landscape,
Emblem and vision,
Loved his margins to fill.

Then might I sit,
By true learning beguiled,
Far into the night
Even with self reconciled,
Retrieving the wisdom
I lost, when a child.

The Last Chapter

I am living more alone now than I did;
This life tends inward, as the body ages;
And what is left of its strange book to read
Quickens in interest with the last few pages.

Problems abound. Its authorship? A sequel?
Its hero-villain, whose ways so little mend?
The plot? Still dark. The style? A shade unequal.
And what of the dénouement? And, the end?

No, no, have done! Lay the thumbed thing aside;
Forget its horrors, folly, incitements, lies;
In silence and in solitude abide,
And con what yet may bless your inward eyes.

Pace, still, for pace with you, companion goes,
Though now, through dulled and inattentive ear,
No more — as when a child's — your sick heart knows
His infinite energy and beauty near.

His, too, a World, though viewless save in glimpse;
He, too, a book of imagery bears;
And, as your halting foot beside him limps,
Mark you whose badge and livery he wears.

The Dove

How often, these hours, have I heard the monotonous crool of a
      dove –
Voice low, insistent, obscure, since its nest it has hid in a
      grove –
Flowers of the linden wherethrough the hosts of the honeybees
      rove.
And I have been busily idle: no problems; nothing to prove;
No urgent foreboding; but only life's shallow habitual groove:
Then why, if I pause to listen, should the languageless note of a
      dove
So dark with disquietude seem? And what is it sorrowing of?

Treachery

She had amid her ringlets bound
Green leaves to rival their dark hue;
How could such locks with beauty bound
      Dry up their dew,
   Wither them through and through?

She had within her dark eyes lit
Sweet fires to burn all doubt away;
Yet did those fires, in darkness lit,
      Burn but a day,
   Not even till twilight stay.

She had within a dusk of words
A vow in simple splendour set;
How, in the memory of such words,
      Could she forget
   That vow – the soul of it?

The Quarry

You hunted me with all the pack,
   Too blind, too blind, to see
By no wild hope of force or greed
   Could you make sure of me.

And like a phantom through the glades,
   With tender breast aglow,
The goddess in me laughed to hear
   Your horns a-roving go.

She laughed to think no mortal ever
   By dint of mortal flesh
The very Cause that was the Hunt
   One moment could enmesh:

That though with captive limbs I lay,
   Stilled breath and vanquished eyes,
He that hunts Love with horse and hound
   Hunts out his heart and eyes.

Incantation

Vervain ... basil ... orison —
Whisper their syllablings till all meaning is gone,
And sound all vestige loses of mere word....
   'Tis then as if, in some far childhood heard,
A wild heart languished at the call of a bird,
Crying through ruinous windows, high and fair,
A secret incantation on the air:
   A language lost; which, when its accents cease,
   Breathes, voiceless, of a pre-Edenic peace.

The Quartette

Tom sang for joy and Ned sang for joy and old Sam sang for
     joy;
All we four boys piped up loud, just like one boy;
And the ladies that sate with the Squire – their cheeks were all
     wet,
For the noise of the voice of us boys, when we sang our
     Quartette.

Tom he piped low and Ned he piped low and old Sam he piped
     low;
Into a sorrowful fall did our music flow;
And the ladies that sate with the Squire vowed they'd never
     forget
How the eyes of them cried for delight, when we sang our
     Quartette.

Tit for Tat

Have you been catching of fish, Tom Noddy?
     Have you snared a weeping hare?
Have you whistled, 'No Nunny,' and gunned a poor bunny,
     Or a blinded bird of the air?

Have you trod like a murderer through the green woods,
     Through the dewy deep dingles and glooms,
While every small creature screamed shrill to Dame Nature,
     'He comes – and he comes!'?

Wonder I very much do, Tom Noddy,
     If ever, when you are a-roam,
An Ogre from space will stoop a lean face,
     And lug you home:

Lug you home over his fence, Tom Noddy,
　　Of thorn-stocks nine yards high,
With your bent knees strung round his old iron gun
　　And your head dan-dangling by:

And hang you up stiff on a hook, Tom Noddy,
　　From a stone-cold pantry shelf,
Whence your eyes will glare in an empty stare,
　　Till you are cooked yourself!

John Masefield

Invocation

O wanderer into many brains,
O spark the emperor's purple hides,
You sow the dusk with fiery grains
When the gold horseman rides.
    O beauty on the darkness hurled,
    Be it through me you shame the world.

Here, the Legion Halted

Here the legion halted, here the ranks were broken,
And the men fell out to gather wood;
And the green wood smoked, and bitter words were spoken,
And the trumpets called to food.

And the sentry on the rampart saw the distance dying
In the smoke of distance blue and far,
And heard the curlew calling and the owl replying
As the night came cold with one star;

And thought of home beyond, over moorland, over marshes,
Over hills, over the sea, across the plains, across the pass,
By a bright sea trodden by the ships of Tarshis,
The farm, with cicadae in the grass.

And thought as I: 'Perhaps, I may be done with living
Tomorrow, when we fight. I shall see those souls no more.
O beloved souls, be beloved in forgiving
The deeds and the words that make me sore.'

Edward Thomas

Tears

It seems I have no tears left. They should have fallen –
Their ghosts, if tears have ghosts, did fall – that day
When twenty hounds streamed by me, not yet combed out
But still all equals in their rage of gladness
Upon the scent, made one, like a great dragon
In Blooming Meadow that bends towards the sun
And once bore hops: and on that other day
When I stepped out from the double-shadowed Tower
Into an April morning, stirring and sweet
And warm. Strange solitude was there and silence.
A mightier charm than any in the Tower
Possessed the courtyard. They were changing guard,
Soldiers in line, young English countrymen,
Fair-haired and ruddy, in white tunics. Drums
And fifes were playing 'The British Grenadiers'.
The men, the music piercing that solitude
And silence, told me truths I had not dreamed,
And have forgotten since their beauty passed.

The Owl

Downhill I came, hungry, and yet not starved;
Cold, yet had heat within me that was proof
Against the North wind; tired, yet so that rest
Had seemed the sweetest thing under a roof.

Then at the inn I had food, fire, and rest,
Knowing how hungry, cold, and tired was I.
All of the night was quite barred out except
An owl's cry, a most melancholy cry

Shaken out long and clear upon the hill,
No merry note, nor cause of merriment,
But one telling me plain what I escaped
And others could not, that night, as in I went.

And salted was my food, and my repose,
Salted and sobered, too, by the bird's voice
Speaking for all who lay under the stars,
Soldiers and poor, unable to rejoice.

Tall Nettles

Tall nettles cover up, as they have done
These many springs, the rusty harrow, the plough
Long worn out, and the roller made of stone:
Only the elm butt tops the nettles now.

This corner of the farmyard I like most:
As well as any bloom upon a flower
I like the dust on the nettles, never lost
Except to prove the sweetness of a shower.

Rain

Rain, midnight rain, nothing but the wild rain
On this bleak hut, and solitude, and me
Remembering again that I shall die

And neither hear the rain nor give it thanks
For washing me cleaner than I have been
Since I was born into this solitude.
Blessed are the dead that the rain rains upon:
But here I pray that none whom I once loved
Is dying tonight or lying still awake
Solitary, listening to the rain,
Either in pain or thus in sympathy
Helpless among the living and the dead,
Like a cold water among broken reeds,
Myriads of broken reeds all still and stiff,
Like me who have no love which this wild rain
Has not dissolved except the love of death,
If love it be for what is perfect and
Cannot, the tempest tells me, disappoint.

Lights Out

I have come to the borders of sleep,
The unfathomable deep
Forest where all must lose
Their way, however straight,
Or winding, soon or late;
They cannot choose.

Many a road and track
That, since the dawn's first crack,
Up to the forest brink,
Deceived the travellers,
Suddenly now blurs,
And in they sink.

Here love ends,
Despair, ambition ends;
All pleasure and all trouble,

Although most sweet or bitter,
Here ends in sleep that is sweeter
Than tasks most noble.

There is not any book
Or face of dearest look
That I would not turn from now
To go into the unknown
I must enter, and leave, alone,
I know not how.

The tall forest towers;
Its cloudy foliage lowers
Ahead, shelf above shelf;
Its silence I hear and obey
That I may lose my way
And myself.

February Afternoon

Men heard this roar of parleying starlings, saw,
  A thousand years ago even as now,
    Black rooks with white gulls following the plough
So that the first are last until a caw
Commands that last are first again, – a law
  Which was of old when one, like me, dreamed how
  A thousand years might dust lie on his brow
Yet thus would birds do between hedge and shaw.

Time swims before me, making as a day
  A thousand years, while the broad ploughland oak
  Roars mill-like and men strike and bear the stroke
  Of war as ever, audacious or resigned,
And God still sits aloft in the array
  That we have wrought him, stone-deaf and stone-blind.

The New House

Now first, as I shut the door,
    I was alone
In the new house; and the wind
    Began to moan.

Old at once was the house,
    And I was old;
My ears were teased with the dread
    Of what was foretold,

Nights of storm, days of mist, without end;
    Sad days when the sun
Shone in vain: old griefs and griefs
    Not yet begun.

All was foretold me; naught
    Could I foresee;
But I learned how the wind would sound
    After these things should be.

Out in the Dark

Out in the dark over the snow
The fallow fawns invisible go
With the fallow doe;
And the winds blow
Fast as the stars are slow.

Stealthily the dark haunts round
And, when the lamp goes, without sound
At a swifter bound
Than the swiftest hound,
Arrives, and all else is drowned;

And star and I and wind and deer,
Are in the dark together, – near,
Yet far, – and fear
Drums on my ear
In that sage company drear.

How weak and little is the light,
All the universe of sight,
Love and delight,
Before the might,
If you love it not, of night.

Harold Monro

Overheard on a Saltmarsh

Nymph, nymph, what are your beads?
Green glass, goblin. Why do you stare at them?
Give them me.
                              No.
Give them me. Give them me.
                              No.
Then I will howl all night in the reeds,
Lie in the mud and howl for them.

Goblin, why do you love them so?

They are better than stars or water,
Better than voices of winds that sing,
Better than any man's fair daughter,
Your green glass beads on a silver ring.

Hush I stole them out of the moon.

Give me your beads, I desire them.
                              No.
I will howl in a deep lagoon
For your green glass beads, I love them so.
Give them me. Give them.
                              No.

James Stephens

The Goat Paths

1

The crooked paths
Go every way
Upon the hill
— They wind about
Through the heather,
In and out
Of a quiet
Sunniness.

And the goats,
Day after day,
Stray
In sunny
Quietness;
Cropping here,
And cropping there
— As they pause,
And turn,
And pass —
Now a bit
Of heather spray,
Now a mouthful
Of the grass.

2

In the deeper
Sunniness;

In the place
Where nothing stirs;
Quietly
In quietness;
In the quiet
Of the furze
They stand a while;
They dream;
They lie;
They stare
Upon the roving sky.

If you approach
They run away!
They will stare,
And stamp,
And bound,
With a sudden angry sound,
To the sunny
Quietude;
To crouch again,
Where nothing stirs,
In the quiet
Of the furze;
To crouch them down again,
And brood,
In the sunny
Solitude.

3

Were I but
As free
As they,
I would stray
Away
And brood;
I would beat

A hidden way,
Through the quiet
Heather spray,
To a sunny
Solitude.

And should you come
I'd run away!
I would make an angry sound,
I would stare,
And stamp,
And bound
To the deeper
Quietude;
To the place
Where nothing stirs
In the quiet
Of the furze.

4

In that airy
Quietness
I would dream
As long as they:
Through the quiet
Sunniness
I would stray
Away
And brood,
All among
The heather spray,
In a sunny
Solitude.

– I would think
Until I found
Something
I can never find;

– Something
Lying
On the ground,
In the bottom
Of my mind.

Nora Criona

I have looked him round and looked him through,
Know everything that he will do

In such a case, and such a case;
And when a frown comes on his face

I dream of it, and when a smile
I trace its sources in a while.

He cannot do a thing but I
Peep to find the reason why;

For I love him, and I seek,
Every evening in the week,

To peep behind his frowning eye
With little query, little pry,

And make him, if a woman can,
Happier than any man.

– Yesterday he gripped her tight
And cut her throat. And serve her right!

Psychometrist

I listened to a man and he
Had no word to say to me:
Then unto a stone I bowed,
And it spoke to me aloud.

– The force that bindeth me so long,
Once sang in the linnet's song;
Now upon the ground I lie,
While the centuries go by!

– Linnets shall for joy atone
And be fastened into stone;
While, upon the waving tree,
Stones shall sing in ecstasy!

The Cherry Tree

Come from your bed, my drowsy gentleman!
And you, fair lady, rise and braid your hair!
And bid the children wash, if that they can;
If not, assist you them, and make them fair
As is the morning, and the morning sky,
And all the sun doth warm in golden air.

For he has climbed the height these times ago!
He laughed among the hills and they were glad;
With bubbled pearl he set the stream aglow
And laced the hedge in silver; and he clad
The lawn in pomp of green, and white, and gold;
And bade the world forget it had been sad.

Then lift yourself, good sir! And you, sweet dame,
Unlash your evening eyes of pious grey!
Call on the children by each lovèd name,
And set them on the grass and bid them play;
And play with them a while, and sing with them,
Beneath the cherry tree, a rondelay.

A Glass of Beer

The lanky hank of a she in the inn over there
Nearly killed me for asking the loan of a glass of beer;
May the devil grip the whey-faced slut by the hair,
And beat bad manners out of her skin for a year.

That parboiled ape, with the toughest jaw you will see
On virtue's path, and a voice that would rasp the dead,
Came roaring and raging the minute she looked at me,
And threw me out of the house on the back of my head!

If I asked her master he'd give me a cask a day;
But she, with the beer at hand, not a gill would arrange!
May she marry a ghost and bear him a kitten, and may
The High King of Glory permit her to get the mange.

Egan O Rahilly

Here in a distant place I hold my tongue;
I am O Rahilly!

When I was young,
Who now am young no more,
I did not eat things picked up from the shore:
The periwinkle, and the tough dog-fish
At even-tide have got into my dish!

The great, where are they now! the great had said —
This is not seemly! Bring to him instead
That which serves his and serves our dignity —
And that was done.

I am O Rahilly!
Here in a distant place he holds his tongue,
Who once said all his say, when he was young!

James Elroy Flecker

To a Poet a Thousand Years Hence

I who am dead a thousand years,
    And wrote this sweet archaic song,
Send you my words for messengers
    The way I shall not pass along.

I care not if you bridge the seas
    Or ride secure the cruel sky,
Or build consummate palaces
    Of metal or of masonry.

But have you wine and music still,
    And statues and a bright-eyed love,
And foolish thoughts of good and ill,
    And prayers to them who sit above?

How shall we conquer? Like a wind
    That falls at eve our fancies blow,
And old Maeonides the blind
    Said it three thousand years ago.

O friend unseen, unborn, unknown,
    Student of our sweet English tongue,
Read out my words at night, alone:
    I was a poet, I was young.

Since I can never see your face,
    And never shake you by the hand,
I send my soul through time and space
    To greet you. You will understand.

Tenebris Interlucentem

A linnet who had lost her way
Sang on a blackened bough in hell,
Till all the ghosts remembered well
The trees, the wind, the golden day.

At last they knew that they had died
When they heard music in that land,
And someone there stole forth a hand
To draw a brother to his side.

J. C. Squire

The Discovery

There was an Indian, who had known no change,
   Who strayed content along a sunlit beach
Gathering shells. He heard a sudden strange
   Commingled noise; looked up; and gasped for speech.
For in the bay, where nothing was before,
   Moved on the sea, by magic, huge canoes,
With bellying cloths on poles, and not one oar,
   And fluttering coloured signs and clambering crews.

And he, in fear, this naked man alone,
   His fallen hands forgetting all their shells,
His lips gone pale, knelt low behind a stone,
   And stared, and saw, and did not understand,
Columbus' doom-burdened caravels
   Slant to the shore, and all their seamen land.

Andrew Young

Sudden Thaw

When day dawned with unusual light,
Hedges in snow stood half their height
And in the white-paved village street
Children were walking without feet.

But now by their own breath kept warm
Muck-heaps are naked at the farm
And even through the shrinking snow
Dead bents and thistles start to grow.

Last Snow

Although the snow still lingers
Heaped on the ivy's blunt webbed fingers
And painting tree-trunks on one side,
Here in this sunlit ride
The fresh unchristened things appear,
Leaf, spathe and stem,
With crumbs of earth clinging to them
To show the way they came
But no flower yet to tell their name,
And one green spear
Stabbing a dead leaf from below
Kills winter at a blow.

A Dead Mole

Strong-shouldered mole,
That so much lived below the ground,
Dug, fought and loved, hunted and fed,
For you to raise a mound
Was as for us to make a hole;
What wonder now that being dead
Your body lies here stout and square
Buried within the blue vault of the air?

Cuckoos

When coltsfoot withers and begins to wear
Long silver locks instead of golden hair,
And fat red catkins from black poplars fall
And on the ground like caterpillars crawl,
And bracken lifts up slender arms and wrists
And stretches them, unfolding sleepy fists,
The cuckoos in a few well-chosen words
Tell they give Easter eggs to the small birds.

The Swallows

All day – when early morning shone
With every dewdrop its own dawn
And when cockchafers were abroad
Hurtling like missiles that had lost their road –

The Swallows twisting here and there
Round unseen corners of the air
Upstream and down so quickly passed
I wondered that their shadows flew as fast.

They steeple-chased over the bridge
And dropped down to a drowning midge
Sharing the river with the fish,
Although the air itself was their chief dish.

Blue-winged snowballs! until they turned
And then with ruddy breasts they burned;
All in one instant everywhere,
Jugglers with their own bodies in the air.

The Beechwood

When the long, varnished buds of beech
Point out beyond their reach,
And tanned by summer suns
Leaves of black bryony turn bronze,
And gossamer floats bright and wet
From trees that are their own sunset,
Spring, summer, autumn I come here,
And what is there to fear?
And yet I never lose the feeling
That someone close behind is stealing
Or else in front has disappeared;
Though nothing I have seen or heard,
The fear of what I might have met
Makes me still walk beneath these boughs
With cautious step as in a haunted house.

The Stones

Though the thick glacier,
That filled the mountain's rocky jaws
And lifted these great rocks like straws
And dropped them here,
Has shrunk to this small ale-brown burn,
Where trout like shadows dart and turn,
The stones in awkward stance
Still wait some starry circumstance
To bring the ice once more
And bear them to a distant shore.

In Teesdale

No, not tonight,
Not by this fading light,
Not by those high fells where the forces
Fall from the mist like the white tails of horses.

From that dark slack
Where peat-hags gape too black
I turn to where the lighted farm
Holds out through the open door a golden arm.

No, not tonight,
Tomorrow by daylight;
Tonight I fear the fabulous horses
Whose white tails flash down the steep watercourses.

Siegfried Sassoon

Counter-Attack

We'd gained our first objective hours before
While dawn broke like a face with blinking eyes,
Pallid, unshaved and thirsty, blind with smoke.
Things seemed all right at first. We held their line,
With bombers posted, Lewis guns well placed,
And clink of shovels deepening the shallow trench.
    The place was rotten with dead; green clumsy legs
    High-booted, sprawled and grovelled along the saps
    And trunks, face downward, in the sucking mud,
    Wallowed like trodden sand-bags loosely filled;
    And naked sodden buttocks, mats of hair,
    Bulged, clotted heads slept in the plastering slime,
    And then the rain began, – the jolly old rain!

A yawning soldier knelt against the bank,
Staring across the morning blear with fog;
He wondered when the Allemands would get busy;
And then, of course, they started with five-nines
Traversing, sure as fate, and never a dud.
Mute in the clamour of shells he watched them burst
Spouting dark earth and wire with gusts from hell,
While posturing giants dissolved in drifts of smoke.
He crouched and flinched, dizzy with galloping fear,
Sick for escape, – loathing the strangled horror
And butchered, frantic gestures of the dead.

An officer came blundering down the trench:
'Stand-to and man the fire-step!' On he went ...
Gasping and bawling, 'Fire-step ... counter-attack!'

Then the haze lifted. Bombing on the right
Down the old sap: Machine-guns on the left;
And stumbling figures looming out in front.
'O Christ, they're coming at us!' Bullets spat,
And he remembered his rifle ... rapid fire ...
And started blazing wildly ... then a bang
Crumpled and spun him sideways, knocked him out
To grunt and wriggle: none heeded him; he choked
And fought the flapping veils of smothering gloom,
Lost in a blurred confusion of yells and groans ...
Down, and down, and down, he sank and drowned,
Bleeding to death. The counter-attack had failed.

'They'

The Bishop tells us: 'When the boys come back
They will not be the same; for they'll have fought
In a just cause: they lead the last attack
On Anti-Christ; their comrades' blood has bought
New right to breed an honourable race,
They have challenged Death and dared him face to face.'

'We're none of us the same!' the boys reply.
'For George lost both his legs; and Bill's stone blind;
Poor Jim's shot through the lungs and like to die;
And Bert's gone syphilitic: you'll not find
A chap who's served that hasn't found *some* change!'
And the Bishop said: 'The ways of God are strange!'

Prelude: The Troops

Dim, gradual thinning of the shapeless gloom
Shudders to drizzling daybreak that reveals
Disconsolate men who stamp their sodden boots
And turn dulled, sunken faces to the sky
Haggard and hopeless. They, who have beaten down
The stale despair of night, must now renew
Their desolation in the truce of dawn,
Murdering the livid hours that grope for peace.

Yet these, who cling to life with stubborn hands,
Can grin through storms of death and find a gap
In the clawed, cruel tangles of his defence.
They march from safety, and the bird-sung joy
Of grass-green thickets, to the land where all
Is ruin, and nothing blossoms but the sky
That hastens over them where they endure
Sad, smoking, flat horizons, reeking woods,
And foundered trench-lines volleying doom for doom.

O my brave brown companions, when your souls
Flock silently away, and the eyeless dead
Shame the wild beast of battle on the ridge,
Death will stand grieving in that field of war
Since your unvanquished hardihood is spent.
And through some mooned Valhalla there will pass
Battalions and battalions, scarred from hell;
The unreturning army that was youth;
The legions who have suffered and are dust.

The Dug-Out

Why do you lie with your legs ungainly huddled,
And one arm bent across your sullen, cold,
Exhausted face? It hurts my heart to watch you,
Deep-shadow'd from the candle's guttering gold;
And you wonder why I shake you by the shoulder;
Drowsy, you mumble and sigh and turn your head ...
You are too young to fall asleep for ever;
And when you sleep you remind me of the dead.

St Venant, July 1918

To any Dead Officer

Well, how are things in Heaven? I wish you'd say,
   Because I'd like to know that you're all right.
Tell me, have you found everlasting day,
   Or been sucked in by everlasting night?
For when I shut my eyes your face shows plain;
   I hear you make some cheery old remark –
I can rebuild you in my brain,
   Though you've gone out patrolling in the dark.

You hated tours of trenches; you were proud
   Of nothing more than having good years to spend;
Longed to get home and join the careless crowd
   Of chaps who work in peace with Time for friend.
That's all washed out now. You're beyond the wire:
   No earthly chance can send you crawling back;
You've finished with machine-gun fire –
   Knocked over in a hopeless dud-attack.

Somehow I always thought you'd get done in,
    Because you were so desperate keen to live:
You were all out to try and save your skin,
    Well knowing how much the world had got to give.
You joked at shells and talked the usual 'shop',
    Stuck to your dirty job and did it fine:
With 'Jesus Christ! when *will* it stop?
    Three years... It's hell unless we break their line.'

So when they told me you'd been left for dead
    I wouldn't believe them, feeling it *must* be true.
Next week the bloody Roll of Honour said
    'Wounded and missing' – (That's the thing to do
When lads are left in shell-holes dying slow,
    With nothing but blank sky and wounds that ache,
Moaning for water till they know
    It's night, and then it's not worth-while to wake!)
        .   .   .   .   .

Good-bye, old lad! Remember me to God,
    And tell him that our Politicians swear
They won't give in till Prussian Rule's been trod
    Under the Heel of England... Are you there?...
Yes... And the War won't end for at least two years;
But we've got stacks of men... I'm blind with tears,
    Staring into the dark. Cheero!
I wished they'd killed you in a decent show.

Memorial Tablet

(Great War)

Squire nagged and bullied till I went to fight,
(Under Lord Derby's Scheme). I died in hell –
(They called it Passchendaele). My wound was slight,
And I was hobbling back; and then a shell
Burst slick upon the duck-boards: so I fell
Into the bottomless mud, and lost the light.

At sermon-time, while Squire is in his pew,
He gives my gilded name a thoughtful stare;
For, though low down upon the list, I'm there;
'*In proud and glorious memory*' ... that's my due.
Two bleeding years I fought in France, for Squire:
I suffered anguish that he's never guessed.
Once I came home on leave: and then went west ...
What greater glory could a man desire?

Aftermath

Have you forgotten yet? ...
For the world's events have rumbled on since those gagged
days,
Like traffic checked awhile at the crossing of city-ways:
And the haunted gap in your mind has filled with thoughts that
flow
Like clouds in the lit heavens of life; and you're a man reprieved
to go,
Taking your peaceful share of Time, with joy to spare.
But the past is just the same – and War's a bloody game ...
Have you forgotten yet? ...
Look down, and swear by the slain of the War that you'll never
forget.

Do you remember the dark months you held the sector at
    Mametz –
The nights you watched and wired and dug and piled sandbags
    on parapets?
Do you remember the rats; and the stench
Of corpses rotting in front of the front-line trench –
And dawn coming, dirty-white, and chill with a hopeless rain?
Do you ever stop and ask, 'Is it all going to happen again?'

Do you remember that hour of din before the attack –
And the anger, the blind compassion that seized and shook you
    then
As you peered at the doomed and haggard faces of your men?
Do you remember the stretcher-cases lurching back
With dying eyes and lolling heads – those ashen-grey
Masks of the lads who once were keen and kind and gay?

Have you forgotten yet? ...
Look up, and swear by the green of the spring that you'll never
    forget.

                                March 1919

Villa d' Este Gardens

'*Of course you saw the Villa d' Este Gardens,*'
  Writes one of my Italianistic friends.
  Of course; of course; I saw them in October,
  Spired with pinaceous ornamental gloom
  Of that arboreal elegy the cypress.

  Those fountains, too, 'like ghosts of cypresses'; –
  (The phrase occurred to me while I was leaning
  On an old balustrade; imbibing sunset;
  Wrapped in my verse vocation) – how they linked me
  With Byron, Landor, Liszt, and Robert Browning! ...

A *liebestraum* of Liszt cajoled my senses.
My language favoured Landor, chaste and formal.
My intellect (though slightly in abeyance)
Functioned against a Byronistic background.
Then Byron jogged my elbow; bade me hob-nob
With some forgotten painter of dim frescoes
That haunt the Villa's intramural twilight.

While roaming in the Villa d'Este Gardens
I felt like that ... and fumbled for my notebook.

Concert-Interpretation

(*Le Sacre du Printemps*)

The Audience pricks an intellectual Ear ...
Stravinsky ... Quite the Concert of the Year!

Forgetting now that none-so-distant date
When they (or folk facsimilar in state
Of mind) first heard with hisses – hoots – guffaws –
The abstract Symphony (they booed because
Stravinsky jumped their Wagner palisade
With modes that seemed cacophonous and queer),
Forgetting now the hullabaloo they made,
The Audience pricks an intellectual ear.

Bassoons begin ... Sonority envelops
Our auditory innocence; and brings
To Me, I must admit, some drift of things
Omnific, seminal, and adolescent.
Polyphony through dissonance develops
A serpent-conscious Eden, crude but pleasant;
While vibro-atmospheric copulations
With mezzo-forte mysteries of noise
Prelude Stravinsky's statement of the joys
That unify the monkeydom of nations.

This matter is most delicate indeed!
Yet one perceives no symptom of stampede.
The Stalls remain unruffled: craniums gleam:
Swept by a storm of pizzicato chords,
Elaborate ladies reassure their lords
With lifting brows that signify 'Supreme!'
While orchestrated gallantry of goats
Impugns the astigmatic programme-notes.

In the Grand Circle one observes no sign
Of riot: peace prevails along the line.
And in the Gallery, cargoed to capacity,
No tremor bodes eruptions and alarms.
They are listening to this not-quite-new audacity
As though it were by someone dead, – like Brahms.

But savagery pervades Me; I am frantic
With corybantic rupturing of Laws.
Come, dance, and seize this clamorous chance to function
Creatively, – abandoning compunction
In anti-social rhapsodic applause!
Lynch the conductor! Jugulate the drums!
Butcher the brass! Ensanguinate the strings!
Throttle the flutes! ... Stravinsky's April comes
With pitiless pomp and pain of sacred springs ...
Incendiarize the Hall with resinous fires
Of sacrificial fiddles scotched and snapping! ...

Meanwhile the music blazes and expires;
And the delighted Audience is clapping.

Rupert Brooke

Sonnet

I said I splendidly loved you; it's not true.
  Such long swift tides stir not a land-locked sea.
On gods or fools the high risk falls – on you –
  The clean clear bitter-sweet that's not for me.
Love soars from earth to ecstasies unwist.
  Love is flung Lucifer-like from heaven to hell.
But – there are wanderers in the middle mist,
  Who cry for shadows, clutch, and cannot tell
Whether they love at all, or, loving, whom:
  An old song's lady, a fool in fancy dress,
Or phantoms, or their own face on the gloom;
  For love of Love, or from heart's loneliness.
Pleasure's not theirs, nor pain. They doubt, and sigh,
And do not love at all. Of these am I.

January 1910

Success

I think if you had loved me when I wanted;
  If I'd looked up one day, and seen your eyes,
And found my wild sick blasphemous prayer granted,
  And your brown face, that's full of pity and wise,
Flushed suddenly; the white godhead in new fear
  Intolerably so struggling, and so shamed;
Most holy and far, if you'd come all too near,
  If earth had seen Earth's lordliest wild limbs tamed,

Shaken, and trapped, and shivering, for *my* touch —
   Myself should I have slain? or that foul you?
But this the strange gods, who had given so much,
   To have seen and known you, this they might not do.
One last shame's spared me, one black word's unspoken;
And I'm alone; and you have not awoken.

                    January 1910

Kindliness

When love has changed to kindliness —
Oh, love, our hungry lips, that press
So tight that Time's an old god's dream
Nodding in heaven, and whisper stuff
Seven million years were not enough
To think on after, make it seem
Less than the breath of children playing,
A blasphemy scarce worth the saying,
A sorry jest, 'When love has grown
To kindliness — to kindliness!' ...
And yet — the best that either's known
Will change, and wither, and be less,
At last, than comfort, or its own
Remembrance. And when some caress
Tendered in habit (once a flame
All heaven sang out to) wakes the shame
Unworded, in the steady eyes
We'll have, — *that* day, what shall we do?
Being so noble, kill the two
Who've reached their second-best? Being wise,
Break cleanly off, and get away,
Follow down other windier skies
New lures, alone? Or shall we stay,
Since this is all we've known, content
In the lean twilight of such day,

And not remember, not lament?
That time when all is over, and
Hand never flinches, brushing hand;
And blood lies quiet, for all you're near;
And it's but spoken words we hear,
Where trumpets sang; when the mere skies
Are stranger and nobler than your eyes;
And flesh is flesh, was flame before;
And infinite hungers leap no more
In the chance swaying of your dress;
And love has changed to kindliness.

Mummia

As those of old drank mummia
    To fire their limbs of lead,
Making dead kings from Africa
    Stand pandar to their bed;

Drunk on the dead, and medicined
    With spiced imperial dust,
In a short night they reeled to find
    Ten centuries of lust.

So I, from paint, stone, tale, and rhyme,
    Stuffed love's infinity,
And sucked all lovers of all time
    To rarefy ecstasy.

Helen's the hair shuts out from me
    Verona's livid skies;
Gypsy the lips I press; and see
    Two Antonys in your eyes.

The unheard invisible lovely dead
   Lie with us in this place,
And ghostly hands above my head
   Close face to straining face;

Their blood is wine along our limbs;
   Their whispering voices wreathe
Savage forgotten drowsy hymns
   Under the names we breathe;

Woven from their tomb, and one with it,
   The night wherein we press;
Their thousand pitchy pyres have lit
   Your flaming nakedness.

For the uttermost years have cried and clung
   To kiss your mouth to mine;
And hair long dust was caught, was flung,
   Hand shaken to hand divine,

And Life has fired, and Death not shaded,
   All Time's uncounted bliss,
And the height o' the world has flamed and faded, –
   Love, that our love be this!

Wagner

Creeps in half wanton, half asleep,
   One with a fat wide hairless face.
He likes love-music that is cheap;
   Likes women in a crowded place;
     And wants to hear the noise they're making.

His heavy eyelids droop half-over,
  Great pouches swing beneath his eyes.
He listens, thinks himself the lover,
  Heaves from his stomach wheezy sighs;
    He likes to feel his heart's a-breaking.

The music swells. His gross legs quiver.
  His little lips are bright with slime.
The music swells. The women shiver.
  And all the while, in perfect time,
    His pendulous stomach hangs a-shaking.

Queen's Hall, 1908

The Song of the Beasts

(Sung, on one night, in the cities, in the darkness)

Come away! Come away!
Ye are sober and dull through the common day,
But now it is night!
It is shameful night, and God is asleep!
(Have you not felt the quick fires that creep
Through the hungry flesh, and the lust of delight,
And hot secrets of dreams that day cannot say?)....
... The house is dumb;
The night calls out to you.... Come, ah, come!
Down the dim stairs, through the creaking door,
Naked, crawling on hands and feet
– It is meet! it is meet!
Ye are men no longer, but less and more,
Beast and God.... Down the lampless street
By little black ways, and secret places,
In darkness and mire,
Faint laughter around, and evil faces

By the star-glint seen – ah! follow with us!
For the darkness whispers a blind desire,
And the fingers of night are amorous....
Keep close as we speed,
Though mad whispers woo you, and hot hands cling,
And the touch and the smell of bare flesh sting,
Soft flank by your flank, and side brushing side –
Tonight never heed!
Unswerving and silent follow with me,
Till the city ends sheer,
And the crook'd lanes open wide,
Out of the voices of night,
Beyond lust and fear,
To the level waters of moonlight,
To the level waters, quiet and clear,
To the black unresting plains of the calling sea.

1906

Safety

Dear! of all happy in the hour, most blest
    He who has found our hid security,
Assured in the dark tides of the world at rest,
    And heard our word, 'Who is so safe as we?'
We have found safety with all things undying,
    The winds, and morning, tears of men and mirth,
The deep night, and birds singing, and clouds flying,
    And sleep, and freedom, and the autumnal earth,

We have built a house that is not for Time's throwing.
    We have gained a peace unshaken by pain for ever.
War knows no power. Safe shall be my going,
    Secretly armed against all death's endeavour;
Safe though all safety's lost; safe where men fall;
And if these poor limbs die, safest of all.

The Soldier

If I should die, think only this of me:
    That there's some corner of a foreign field
That is for ever England. There shall be
    In that rich earth a richer dust concealed;
A dust whom England bore, shaped, made aware,
    Gave, once, her flowers to love, her ways to roam,
A body of England's, breathing English air,
    Washed by the rivers, blest by suns of home.

And think, this heart, all evil shed away,
    A pulse in the eternal mind, no less
        Gives somewhere back the thoughts by England given;
Her sights and sounds; dreams happy as her day;
    And laughter, learnt of friends; and gentleness,
        In hearts at peace, under an English heaven.

Ivor Gurney

Townshend

Townshend? I knew him well, queer ways he had.
Fond of plays, fond of books, and of Roman talk,
Campments, marches, *pila* and a mix of relics
Found by western folk in a casual walk.
A quick man in his talk, with eyes always sad.
Kind? Yes, and honourer of poets and actor folk.
Chettle and Heywood ... but most Jonson he loved.
Angry with London for neglect that so evil proved
Who lived two years with him and was great labourer
As 'Cataline' and many other things to which he was moved
Showed; he read much Latin, and was proud of Greek,
Townshend would leave him whole days alone in his house
And go to Surrey or Buckingham and take delight,
Or watch Danbury changing in the March light.
Knowing Jonson labouring like the great son he was
Of Solway and of Westminster – O, maker, maker,
Given of all the gods to anything but grace.
And kind as all the apprentices knew and scholars;
A talker with battle honours till dawn whitened the curtains,
With many honourers, and many, many enemies, and followers.

There's one said to me 'I love his face,
But if he smites me flat for a false Greek quantity,
And drinks a quart where I should be trembler and shaker,
It must be said, "I love him". He does me disgrace
And I shall pay him back for the sight of posterity
For all great Cataline and Alchemist its high play,
Unless he loves me more or I have greater charity.'

Robecq Again

Robecq had straw and a comfortable tavern
Where men might their sinews feel slowly recovering
From the march-strain, and there was autumn's translucence
In the calm air and a tang of the earth and its essence.
A girl served wine there with natural dignity
Moving as any princess from care free,
And the north French air bathed crystal the flat land
With cabbages and tobacco plants and varied culture spanned.
Beautiful with moist clarity of autumn's breath.
Lovely with the year's turning to leafless death.
Robecq, the dark town at night with *estaminets* lit,
The outside roads with poplars, plane trees on it,
Huge dark barn with candles throwing warning flares,
Glooms steady and shifting pierced with cold flowing airs,
With dumb peace at last and a wrapping from cares.
'O Margaret, your music served me. I also made beauty.'

Victoria Sackville-West

Full Moon

She was wearing the coral taffeta trousers
Someone had brought her from Ispahan,
And the little gold coat with pomegranate blossoms,
And the coral-hafted feather fan;
But she ran down a Kentish lane in the moonlight,
And skipped in the pool of the moon as she ran.

She cared not a rap for all the big planets,
For Betelgeuse or Aldebaran,
And all the big planets cared nothing for her,
That small impertinent charlatan;
But she climbed on a Kentish stile in the moonlight,
And laughed at the sky through the sticks of her fan.

Wilfred Owen

Arms and the Boy

Let the boy try along this bayonet-blade
How cold steel is, and keen with hunger of blood;
Blue with all malice, like a madman's flash;
And thinly drawn with famishing for flesh.

Lend him to stroke these blind, blunt bullet-heads
Which long to nuzzle in the hearts of lads,
Or give him cartridges of fine zinc teeth,
Sharp with the sharpness of grief and death.

For his teeth seem for laughing round an apple.
There lurk no claws behind his fingers supple;
And God will grow no talons at his heels,
Nor antlers through the thickness of his curls.

The Show

> We have fallen in the dreams the ever-living
> Breathe on the tarnished mirror of the world,
> And then smooth out with ivory hands and sigh.
> W. B. YEATS

My soul looked down from a vague height, with Death,
As unremembering how I rose or why,
And saw a sad land, weak with sweats of dearth,
Gray, cratered like the moon with hollow woe,
And pitted with great pocks and scabs of plagues.

Across its beard, that horror of harsh wire,
There moved thin caterpillars, slowly uncoiled.
It seemed they pushed themselves to be as plugs
Of ditches, where they writhed and shrivelled, killed.

By them had slimy paths been trailed and scraped
Round myriad warts that might be little hills.

From gloom's last dregs these long-strung creatures crept,
And vanished out of dawn down hidden holes.

(And smell came up from those foul openings
As out of mouths, or deep wounds deepening.)

On dithering feet upgathered, more and more,
Brown strings, towards strings of gray, with bristling spines,
All migrants from green fields, intent on mire.

Those that were gray, of more abundant spawns,
Ramped on the rest and ate them and were eaten.

I saw their bitten backs curve, loop, and straighten,
I watched those agonies curl, lift, and flatten.
Whereat, in terror what that sight might mean,
I reeled and shivered earthward like a feather.

And Death fell with me, like a deepening moan.
And he, picking a manner of worm, which half had hid
Its bruises in the earth, but crawled no further,
Showed me its feet, the feet of many men,
And the fresh-severed head of it, my head.

Dulce et Decorum Est

Bent double, like old beggars under sacks,
Knock-kneed, coughing like hags, we cursed through sludge,
Till on the haunting flares we turned our backs
And towards our distant rest began to trudge.
Men marched asleep. Many had lost their boots
But limped on, blood-shod. All went lame; all blind;
Drunk with fatigue; deaf even to the hoots
Of tired, outstripped Five-Nines that dropped behind.

Gas! GAS! Quick, boys! – An ecstasy of fumbling,
Fitting the clumsy helmets just in time;
But someone still was yelling out and stumbling
And flound'ring like a man in fire or lime. –
Dim, through the misty panes and thick green light,
As under a green sea, I saw him drowning.

In all my dreams, before my helpless sight,
He plunges at me, guttering, choking, drowning.

If in some smothering dreams, you too could pace
Behind the wagon that we flung him in,
And watch the white eyes writhing in his face,
His hanging face, like a devil's sick of sin;
If you could hear, at every jolt, the blood
Come gargling from the froth-corrupted lungs,
Obscene as cancer, bitter as the cud
Of vile, incurable sores on innocent tongues, –
My friend, you would not tell with such high zest
To children ardent for some desperate glory,
The old Lie: Dulce et decorum est
Pro patria mori.

The Dead-Beat

He dropped, – more sullenly than wearily,
Lay stupid like a cod, heavy like meat,
And none of us could kick him to his feet;
Just blinked at my revolver, blearily;
– Didn't appear to know a war was on,
Or see the blasted trench at which he stared.
'I'll do 'em in,' he whined. 'If this hand's spared,
I'll murder them, I will.'
              A low voice said,
'It's Blighty, p'raps, he sees; his pluck's all gone,
Dreaming of all the valiant, that aren't dead:
Bold uncles, smiling ministerially;
Maybe his brave young wife, getting her fun
In some new home, improved materially.
It's not these stiffs have crazed him; nor the Hun.'

We sent him down at last, out of the way.
Unwounded; – stout lad, too, before that strafe.
Malingering? Stretcher-béarers winked, 'Not half!'

Next day I heard the Doc.'s well-whiskied laugh:
'That scum you sent last night soon died. Hooray.'

Mental Cases

Who are these? Why sit they here in twilight?
Wherefore rock they, purgatorial shadows,
Drooping tongues from jaws that slob their relish,
Baring teeth that leer like skulls' teeth wicked?
Stroke on stroke of pain, – but what slow panic
Gouged these chasms round their fretted sockets?
Ever from their hair and through their hands' palms
Misery swelters. Surely we have perished
Sleeping, and walk hell; but who these hellish?

– These are men whose minds the Dead have ravished.
Memory fingers in their hair of murders,
Multitudinous murders they once witnessed.
Wading sloughs of flesh these helpless wander,
Treading blood from lungs that had loved laughter.
Always they must see these things and hear them,
Batter of guns and shatter of flying muscles,
Carnage incomparable, and human squander
Rucked too thick for these men's extrication.

Therefore still their eyeballs shrink tormented
Back into their brains, because on their sense
Sunlight seems a blood-smear; night comes blood-black;
Dawn breaks open like a wound that bleeds afresh,
– Thus their heads wear this hilarious, hideous,
Awful falseness of set-smiling corpses.
– Thus their hands are plucking at each other;
Picking at the rope-knouts of their scourging;
Snatching after us who smote them, brother,
Pawing us who dealt them war and madness.

Futility

Move him into the sun –
Gently its touch awoke him once,
At home, whispering of fields unsown.
Always it woke him, even in France,
Until this morning and this snow.
If anything might rouse him now
The kind old sun will know.

Think how it wakes the seeds, –
Woke, once, the clays of a cold star.
Are limbs, so dear-achieved, are sides,
Full-nerved – still warm – too hard to stir?

Was it for this the clay grew tall?
– O what made fatuous sunbeams toil
To break earth's sleep at all?

Anthem for Doomed Youth

What passing-bells for these who die as cattle?
    Only the monstrous anger of the guns.
    Only the stuttering rifles' rapid rattle
Can patter out their hasty orisons.
No mockeries now for them; no prayers nor bells,
    Nor any voice of mourning save the choirs, –
The shrill, demented choirs of wailing shells;
    And bugles calling for them from sad shires.

What candles may be held to speed them all?
    Not in the hands of boys, but in their eyes
Shall shine the holy glimmers of good-byes.
    The pallor of girls' brows shall be their pall;
Their flowers the tenderness of patient minds,
And each slow dusk a drawing-down of blinds.

Apologia Pro Poemate Meo

I, too, saw God through mud, –
    The mud that cracked on cheeks when wretches smiled.
    War brought more glory to their eyes than blood,
    And gave their laughs more glee than shakes a child.

Merry it was to laugh there –
    Where death becomes absurd and life absurder.
    For power was on us as we slashed bones bare
    Not to feel sickness or remorse of murder.

I, too, have dropped off fear —
    Behind the barrage, dead as my platoon,
    And sailed my spirit surging light and clear
    Past the entanglement where hopes lay strewn;

And witnessed exultation —
    Faces that used to curse me, scowl for scowl,
    Shine and lift up with passion of oblation,
    Seraphic for an hour; though they were foul.

I have made fellowships —
    Untold of happy lovers in old song.
    For love is not the binding of fair lips
    With the soft silk of eyes that look and long,

By Joy, whose ribbon slips, —
    But wound with war's hard wire whose stakes are strong;
    Bound with the bandage of the arm that drips;
    Knit in the webbing of the rifle-thong.

I have perceived much beauty
    In the hoarse oaths that kept our courage straight;
    Heard music in the silentness of duty;
    Found peace where shell-storms spouted reddest spate.

Nevertheless, except you share
    With them in hell the sorrowful dark of hell,
    Whose world is but the trembling of a flare,
    And heaven but as the highway for a shell,

You shall not hear their mirth:
    You shall not come to think them well content
    By any jest of mine. These men are worth
    Your tears. You are not worth their merriment.

                          November 1917

Hospital Barge at Cérisy

Budging the sluggard ripples of the Somme,
A barge round old Cérisy slowly slewed.
Softly her engines down the current screwed
And chuckled in her, with contented hum.

Till fairy tinklings struck their croonings dumb.
The waters rumpling at the stern subdued.
The lock-gate took her bulging amplitude.
Gently from out the gurgling lock she swum.

One reading by that sunset raised his eyes
To watch her lessening westward quietly,
Till, as she neared the bend, her funnel screamed.

And that long lamentation made him wise
How unto Avalon, in agony,
Kings passed in the dark barge, which Merlin dreamed.

                                    8 December 1917

Miners

There was a whispering in my hearth,
    A sigh of the coal,
Grown wistful of a former earth
    It might recall.

I listened for a tale of leaves
    And smothered ferns;
Frond-forests; and the low, sly lives
    Before the fawns.

My fire might show steam-phantoms simmer
    From Time's old cauldron;
Before the birds made nests in summer,
    Or men had children.

But the coals were murmuring of their mine,
   And moans down there
Of boys that slept wry sleep, and men
   Writhing for air.

And I saw white bones in the cinder-shard.
   Bones without number;
For many hearts with coal are charred
   And few remember.

I thought of some who worked dark pits
   Of war, and died
Digging the rock where Death reputes
   Peace lies indeed.

Comforted years will sit soft-chaired
   In rooms of amber;
The years will stretch their hands, well-cheered
   By our lives' ember.

The centuries will burn rich loads
   With which we groaned,
Whose warmth shall lull their dreaming lids
   While songs are crooned.
But they will not dream of us poor lads
   Lost in the ground.

Spring Offensive

Halted against the shade of a last hill,
They fed, and, lying easy, were at ease
And, finding comfortable chests and knees,
Carelessly slept. But many there stood still
To face the stark, blank sky beyond the ridge,
Knowing their feet had come to the end of the world.

Marvelling they stood, and watched the long grass swirled
By the May breeze, murmurous with wasp and midge,
For though the summer oozed into their veins
Like an injected drug for their bodies' pains,
Sharp on their souls hung the imminent line of grass,
Fearfully flashed the sky's mysterious glass.

Hour after hour they ponder the warm field –
And the far valley behind, where the buttercup
Had blessed with gold their slow boots coming up,
Where even the little brambles would not yield,
But clutched and clung to them like sorrowing hands;
They breathe like trees unstirred.

Till like a cold gust thrills the little word
At which each body and its soul begird
And tighten them for battle. No alarms
Of bugles, no high flags, no clamorous haste –
Only a lift and flare of eyes that faced
The sun, like a friend with whom their love is done.
O larger shone that smile against the sun, –
Mightier than his whose bounty these have spurned.

So, soon they topped the hill, and raced together
Over an open stretch of herb and heather
Exposed. And instantly the whole sky burned
With fury against them; earth set sudden cups
In thousands for their blood; and the green slope
Chasmed and steepened sheer to infinite space.

.   .   .   .   .

Of them who running on that last high place
Leapt to swift unseen bullets, or went up
On the hot blast and fury of hell's upsurge,
Or plunged and fell away past this world's verge,
Some say God caught them even before they fell.

But what say such as from existence' brink
Ventured but drave too swift to sink,
The few who rushed in the body to enter hell,
And there out-fiending all its fiends and flames
With superhuman inhumanities,
Long-famous glories, immemorial shames –
And crawling slowly back, have by degrees
Regained cool peaceful air in wonder –
Why speak not they of comrades that went under?

Strange Meeting

It seemed that out of battle I escaped
Down some profound dull tunnel, long since scooped
Through granites which titanic wars had groined.
Yet also there encumbered sleepers groaned,
Too fast in thought or death to be bestirred.
Then, as I probed them, one sprang up, and stared
With piteous recognition in fixed eyes,
Lifting distressful hands as if to bless.
And by his smile, I knew that sullen hall,
By his dead smile I knew we stood in Hell.
With a thousand pains that vision's face was grained;
Yet no blood reached there from the upper ground,
And no guns thumped, or down the flues made moan.
'Strange friend,' I said, 'here is no cause to mourn.'
'None,' said that other, 'save the undone years,
The hopelessness. Whatever hope is yours,
Was my life also; I went hunting wild
After the wildest beauty in the world,
Which lies not calm in eyes, or braided hair,
But mocks the steady running of the hour,
And if it grieves, grieves richlier than here.
For of my glee might many men have laughed,
And of my weeping something had been left,

Which must die now. I mean the truth untold,
The pity of war, the pity war distilled.
Now men will go content with what we spoiled,
Or, discontent, boil bloody, and be spilled.
They will be swift with swiftness of the tigress.
None will break ranks, though nations trek from progress.
Courage was mine, and I had mystery,
Wisdom was mine, and I had mastery:
To miss the march of this retreating world
Into vain citadels that are not walled.
Then, when much blood had clogged their chariot wheels,
I would go up and wash them from sweet wells,
Even with truths that lie too deep for taint.
I would have poured my spirit without stint
But not through wounds; not on the cess of war.
Foreheads of men have bled where no wounds were.
I am the enemy you killed, my friend.
I knew you in this dark: for so you frowned
Yesterday through me as you jabbed and killed.
I parried; but my hands were loath and cold.
Let us sleep now. ...'

Robert Graves

The Morning Before the Battle

Today, the fight: my end is very soon,
    And sealed the warrant limiting my hours:
I knew it walking yesterday at noon
    Down a deserted garden full of flowers.
... Carelessly sang, pinned roses on my breast,
    Reached for a cherry-bunch – and then, then, **Death**
Blew through the garden from the north and east
    And blighted every beauty with chill breath.

I looked, and ah my wraith before me stood,
    His head all battered in by violent blows:
The fruit between my lips to clotted blood
    Was transubstantiate, and the pale rose
Smelt sickly, till it seemed through a swift tear-flood
    That dead men blossomed in the garden-close.

I Hate the Moon

I hate the Moon, though it makes most people glad,
    And they giggle and talk of silvery beams – you know!
But *she* says the look of the Moon drives people mad,
    And that's the thing that always frightens me so.

I hate it worst when it's cruel and round and bright,
    And you can't make out the marks on its stupid face,
Except when you shut your eyelashes, and all night
    The sky looks green, and the world's a horrible place.

129

I like the stars, and especially the Big Bear
    And the W star, and one like a diamond ring,
But I *hate* the Moon and its horrible stony stare,
    And I know one day it'll do me some dreadful thing.

Big Words

'I've whined of coming death, but now no more!
It's weak and most ungracious. For, say I,
Though still a boy if years are counted, why!
I've lived those years from roof to cellar-floor,
And feel, like grey-beards touching their fourscore,
Ready, so soon as the need comes, to die:
    And I'm satisfied.
For winning confidence in those quiet days
Of peace, poised sickly on the precipice side
Of Lliwedd crag by Snowdon, and in war
Finding it firmlier with me than before;
Winning a faith in the wisdom of God's ways
That once I lost, finding it justified
Even in this chaos; winning love that stays
And warms the heart like wine at Easter-tide;
    Having earlier tried
False loves in plenty; oh! my cup of praise
Brims over, and I know I'll feel small sorrow,
Confess no sins and make no weak delays
If death ends all and I must die tomorrow.'

But on the firestep, waiting to attack
He cursed, prayed, sweated, wished the proud words back.

Goliath and David

(For D.C.T., killed at Fricourt, March 1916)

Once an earlier David took
Smooth pebbles from the brook:
Out between the lines he went
To that one-sided tournament,
A shepherd boy who stood out fine
And young to fight a Philistine
Clad all in brazen mail. He swears
That he's killed lions, he's killed bears,
And those that scorn the God of Zion
Shall perish so like bear or lion.
But ... the historian of that fight
Had not the heart to tell it right.

Striding within javelin range
Goliath marvels at this strange
Goodly faced boy so proud of strength.
David's clear eye measures the length;
With hand thrust back, he cramps one knee,
Poises a moment thoughtfully,
And hurls with a long vengeful swing.
The pebble, humming from the sling
Like a wild bee, flies a sure line
For the forehead of the Philistine;
Then ... but there comes a brazen clink,
And quicker than a man can think
Goliath's shield parries each cast.
Clang! clang! and clang! was David's last.
Scorn blazes in the Giant's eye,
Towering unhurt six cubits high.
Says foolish David, 'Damn your shield!
And damn my sling! but I'll not yield.'
He takes his staff of Mamre oak,
A knotted shepherd-staff that's broke
The skull of many a wolf and fox

Come filching lambs from Jesse's flocks.
Loud laughs Goliath, and that laugh
Can scatter chariots like blown chaff
To rout: but David, calm and brave,
Holds his ground, for God will save.
Steel crosses wood, a flash, and oh!
Shame for beauty's overthrow!
(God's eyes are dim, his ears are shut.)
One cruel backhand sabre cut –
'I'm hit! I'm killed!' young David cries,
Throws blindly forward, chokes ... and dies.

And look, spike-helmeted, grey, grim,
Goliath straddles over him.

A Boy in Church

'Gabble-gabble ... brethren ... gabble-gabble!'
    My window glimpses larch and heather.
I hardly hear the tuneful babble,
    Not knowing nor much caring whether
The text is praise or exhortation,
Prayer or thanksgiving or damnation.

Outside it blows wetter and wetter,
    The tossing trees never stay still;
I shift my elbows to catch better
    The full round sweep of heathered hill.
The tortured copse bends to and fro
In silence like a shadow-show.

The parson's voice runs like a river
    Over smooth rocks. I like this church.
The pews are staid, they never shiver,
    They never bend or sway or lurch.
'Prayer', says the kind voice, 'is a chain
That draws down Grace from heaven again.'

I add the hymns up over and over
   Until there's not the least mistake.
Seven-seventy-one. (Look! there's a plover!
   It's gone!) Who's that Saint by the Lake?
The red light from his mantle passes
Across the broad memorial brasses.

.   .   .   .   .

It's pleasant here for dreams and thinking,
   Lolling and letting reason nod,
With ugly, serious people thinking
   Prayer-chains for a forgiving God.
But a dumb blast sets the trees swaying
With furious zeal like madmen praying.

A Lover since Childhood

Tangled in thought am I,
Stumble in speech do I,
Do I blunder and blush for the reason why?
Wander aloof do I,
Lean over gates and sigh,
Making friends with the bee and the butterfly?

If thus and thus I do,
Dazed by the thought of you,
Walking my sorrowful way in the early dew,
My heart cut through and through
In this despair for you,
Starved for a word or a look will my hope renew;

Give then a thought for me
Walking so miserably,
Wanting relief in the friendship of flower or tree;
Do but remember, we
Once could in love agree,
Swallow your pride, let us be as we used to be.

Outlaws

Owls – they whinny down the night;
   Bats go zigzag by.
Ambushed in shadow beyond sight
   The outlaws lie.

Old gods, tamed to silence, there
   In the wet woods they lurk,
Greedy of human stuff to snare
   In nets of murk.

Look up, else your eye will drown
   In a moving sea of black;
Between the tree-tops, upside down,
   Goes the sky-track.

Look up, else your feet will stray
   Into that ambuscade
Where spider-like they trap their prey
   With webs of shade.

For though creeds whirl away in dust,
   Faith dies and men forget,
These agèd gods of power and lust
   Cling to life yet –

Old gods almost dead, malign,
   Starving for unpaid dues:
Incense and fire, salt, blood and wine
   And a drumming muse,

Banished to woods and a sickly moon,
   Shrunk to mere bogey things,
Who spoke with thunder once at noon
   To prostrate kings:

With thunder from an open sky
 To warrior, virgin, priest,
Bowing in fear with a dazzled eye
 Toward the dread East —

Proud gods, humbled, sunk so low,
 Living with ghosts and ghouls,
And ghosts of ghosts and last year's snow
 And dead toadstools.

The Haunted House

'Come, surly fellow, come: a song!'
 What, fools? Sing to you?
Choose from the clouded tales of wrong
 And terror I bring to you:

Of a night so torn with cries,
 Honest men sleeping
Start awake with rabid eyes,
 Bone-chilled, flesh creeping,

Of spirits in the web-hung room
 Up above the stable,
Groans, knockings in the gloom,
 The dancing table,

Of demons in the dry well
 That cheep and mutter,
Clanging of an unseen bell,
 Blood choking the gutter,

Of lust frightful past belief
 Lurking unforgotten,
Unrestrainable endless grief
 In breasts long rotten.

A song? What laughter or what song
  Can this house remember?
Do flowers and butterflies belong
  To a blind December?

The Leveller

Near Martinpuisch that night of hell
Two men were struck by the same shell,
Together tumbling in one heap
Senseless and limp like slaughtered sheep.

One was a pale eighteen-year-old,
Girlish and thin and not too bold,
Pressed for the war ten years too soon,
The shame and pity of his platoon.

The other came from far-off lands
With bristling chin and whiskered hands,
He had known death and hell before
In Mexico and Ecuador.

Yet in his death this cut-throat wild
Groaned 'Mother! Mother!' like a child,
While that poor innocent in man's clothes
Died cursing God with brutal oaths.

Old Sergeant Smith, kindest of men,
Wrote out two copies there and then
Of his accustomed funeral speech
To cheer the womenfolk of each.

Lost Love

His eyes are quickened so with grief,
He can watch a grass or leaf
Every instant grow; he can
Clearly through a flint wall see,
Or watch the startled spirit flee
From the throat of a dead man.
    Across two counties he can hear
And catch your words before you speak.
The woodlouse or the maggot's weak
Clamour rings in his sad ear,
And noise so slight it would surpass
Credence – drinking sound of grass,
Worm talk, clashing jaws of moth
Chumbling holes in cloth;
The groan of ants who undertake
Gigantic loads for honour's sake
(Their sinews creak, their breath comes thin);
Whir of spiders when they spin,
And minute whispering, mumbling, sighs
Of idle grubs and flies.
    This man is quickened so with grief,
He wanders god-like or like thief
Inside and out, below, above,
Without relief seeking lost love.

A History of Peace

(*Solitudinem faciunt, pacem appellant*)

Here rest in peace the bones of Henry Reece,
Dead through his bitter championship of Peace
Against all eagle-nosed and cynic lords
Who keep the Pax Romana with their swords.
Henry was only son of Thomas Reece,
Banker and sometime Justice of the Peace,
And of Jane Reece whom Thomas kept in dread
By Pax Romana of his board and bed.

Dead Boche

To you who read my songs of war
    And only hear of blood and fame,
I'll say (you've heard it said before)
    'War's Hell!' and if you doubt the same,
Today I found in Mametz Wood
A certain cure for lust of blood:

Where, propped against a shattered trunk,
    In a great mess of things unclean,
Sat a dead Boche; he scowled and stunk
    With clothes and face a sodden green,
Big-bellied, spectacled, crop-haired,
Dribbling black blood from nose and beard.

Charles Sorley

To Poets

We are the homeless, even as you,
Who hope and never can begin.
Our hearts are wounded through and through
Like yours, but our hearts bleed within.
We too make music, but our tones
'Scape not the barrier of our bones.

We have no comeliness like you.
We toil, unlovely, and we spin.
We start, return: we wind, undo:
We hope, we err, we strive, we sin,
We love: your love's not greater, but
The lips of our love's might stay shut.

We have the evil spirits too
That shake our soul with battle-din.
But we have an eviller spirit than you,
We have a dumb spirit within:
The exceeding bitter agony
But not the exceeding bitter cry.

September 1914

German Rain

The heat came down and sapped away my powers.
The laden heat came down and drowsed my brain,
Till through the weight of overcoming hours
          I felt the rain.

Then suddenly I saw what more to see
I never thought: old things renewed, retrieved.
The rain that fell in England fell on me,
          And I believed.

Rooks

There, where the rusty iron lies,
    The rooks are cawing all the day.
Perhaps no man, until he dies,
    Will understand them, what they say.

The evening makes the sky like clay.
    The slow wind waits for night to rise.
The world is half-content. But they

Still trouble all the trees with cries,
    That know, and cannot put away,
The yearning to the soul that flies
    From day to night, from night to day.

                              21 June 1913

Edmund Blunden

Malefactors

Nailed to these green laths long ago,
You cramp and shrivel into dross,
Blotched with mildews, gnawed with moss,
And now the eye can scarcely know
The snake among you from the kite,
   So sharp does Death's fang bite.

I guess your stories; you were shot
Hovering above the miller's chicks;
And you, coiled on his threshold bricks –
Hissing you died; and you, sir Stoat,
Dazzled with stablemen's lantern stood
   And tasted crabtree wood.

Here then you leered-at luckless churls,
Clutched to your clumsy gibbet, shrink
To shapeless orts; hard by the brink
Of this black scowling pond that swirls
To turn the wheel beneath the mill,
   The wheel so long since still.

There's your revenge, the wheel at tether,
The miller gone, the white planks rotten,
The very name of the mill forgotten,
Dimness and silence met together.
Felons of fur and feather, can
   There lurk some crime in man,

In man your executioner,
Whom here Fate's cudgel battered down?
Did he too filch from squire and clown?
The damp gust makes the ivy whirr
Like passing death; the sluices well,
    Dreary as a passing-bell.

Winter: East Anglia

In a frosty sunset
    So fiery red with cold
The footballers' onset
    Rings out glad and bold;
Then boys from daily tether
    With famous dogs at heel
In starlight meet together
    And to farther hedges steal;
Where the rats are pattering
    In and out the stacks,
Owls with hatred chattering
    Swoop at the terriers' backs.
And, frost forgot, the chase grows hot
    Till a rat's a foolish prize,
But the cornered weasel stands his ground,
Shrieks at the dogs and boys set round,
Shrieks as he knows they stand all round,
    And hard as winter dies.

The Midnight Skaters

The hop-poles stand in cones,
    The icy pond lurks under,
The pole-tops steeple to the thrones
    Of stars, sound gulfs of wonder;
But not the tallest there, 'tis said,
Could fathom to the pond's black bed.

Then is not death at watch
    Within those secret waters?
What wants he but to catch
    Earth's heedless sons and daughters?
With but a crystal parapet
Between, he has his engines set.

Then on, blood shouts, on, on,
    Twirl, wheel and whip above him,
Dance on this ball-floor thin and wan,
    Use him as though you love him;
Court him, elude him, reel and pass,
And let him hate you through the glass.

Concert-Party: Busseboom

The stage was set, the house was packed,
    The famous troop began;
Our laughter thundered, act by act;
    Time light as sunbeams ran.

Dance sprang and spun and neared and fled,
    Jest chirped at gayest pitch,
Rhythm dazzled, action sped
    Most comically rich.

With generals and lame privates both
    Such charms worked wonders, till
The show was over – lagging loth
    We faced the sunset chill;

And standing on the sandy way,
    With the cracked church peering past,
We heard another matinée,
    We heard the maniac blast

Of barrage south by Saint Éloi,
    And the red lights flaming there
Called madness: Come, my bonny boy,
    And dance to the latest air.

To this new concert, white we stood;
    Cold certainty held our breath;
While men in the tunnels below Larch Wood
    Were kicking men to death.

The Prophet

It is a country,
Says this old guide-book to the Netherlands,
– Written when Waterloo was hardly over,
And justified 'a warmer interest
In English travellers' – Flanders is a country
Which, boasting not 'so many natural beauties'
As others, yet has history enough.
I like the book; it flaunts the polished phrase
Which our forefathers practised equally
To bury admirals or sell beaver hats;
Let me go on, and note you here and there
Words with a difference to the likes of us.

'The author will not dwell on the temptations
Which many parts of Belgium offer'; he
'Will not insist on the salubrity
Of the air.' I thank you, sir, for those few words.
With which we find ourselves in sympathy.
And here are others: 'here the unrivalled skill
Of British generals, and the British soldier's
Unconquerable valour ...' no, not us.
Proceed.
'The necessary cautions on the road' ...
Gas helmets at the alert, no daylight movement?
'But lately much attention has been paid
To the coal mines.' Amen, roars many a fosse
Down south, and slag-heap unto slag-heap calls.
'The Flemish farmers are likewise distinguished
For their attention to manure.' Perchance.
First make your mixen, then about it raise
Your tenements; let the house and sheds and sties
And arch triumphal opening on the mud
Inclose that Mecca in a square. The fields,
Our witness saith, are for the most part small,
And 'leases are unfortunately short'.
In this again perceive veracity;
At Zillebeke the cultivator found
That it was so; and Fritz, who thought to settle
Down by the Verbrandenmolen, came with spades,
And dropped his spades, and ran more dead than alive.
Nor, to disclose a secret, do I languish
For lack of a long lease on Pilkem Ridge.

While in these local haunts, I cannot wait
But track the author on familiar ground.
He comes from Menin, names the village names
That since rang round the world, leaves Zillebeke,
Crosses a river (so he calls that blood-leat
Bassevillebeek), a hill (a hideous hill),
And reaches Ypres, 'a pleasant, well-built town'.

My Belgian Traveller, did no threatening whisper
Sigh to you from the hid profound of fate
Ere you passed thence, and noted 'Poperinghe.
Traffic in serge and hops'? (The words might still
Convey sound fact.) Perhaps some dim hush envoy
Entered your spirit when at Furnes you wrote,
'The air is reckoned unhealthy here for strangers.'
I find your pen as driven by irony's fingers,
Defend the incorrectness of your map
With this: it was not fitting to delay,
Though 'in a few weeks a new treaty of Paris
Would render it useless'. Good calm worthy man,
I leave you changing horses, and I wish you
Good *blanc* at Nieuport. – Truth did not disdain
This sometime seer, crass but Cassandra-like.

Trust

    Trust is a trembling thing;
No glaring champion never overthrown,
No cannon grinning out of catacombed stone,
But a young sparrow that with just-tried wing
On some steep wall-face fluttering goes to cling;
Or a petticoated child not two years old,
Who with a simple-simulated wrath
Bids some great dog begone out of his path,
    Betwixt abashed and bold.

My pretty fledgeling, flit and light unlamed,
Can Nature else but love you? Shrilly berate
That slow old dog, young darling; it was foretold
    You should not be ashamed
So speaking with your enemies in the gate.

Report on Experience

I have been young, and now am not too old;
And I have seen the righteous forsaken,
His health, his honour and his quality taken.
    This is not what we were formerly told.

I have seen a green country, useful to the race,
Knocked silly with guns and mines, its villages vanished,
Even the last rat and last kestrel banished –
    God bless us all, this was peculiar grace.

I knew Seraphina; Nature gave her hue,
Glance, sympathy, note, like one from Eden.
I saw her smile warp, heard her lyric deaden;
    She turned to harlotry; – this I took to be new.

Say what you will, our God sees how they run.
These disillusions are His curious proving
That he loves humanity and will go on loving;
    Over there are faith, life, virtue in the sun.

The Sunlit Vale

I saw the sunlit vale, and the pastoral fairy-tale;
The sweet and bitter scent of the may drifted by;
And never have I seen such a bright bewildering green,
    But it looked like a lie,
    Like a kindly meant lie.

When gods are in dispute, one a Sidney, one a brute,
It would seem that human sense might not know, might not
    spy;
But though nature smile and feign where foul play has stabbed
    and slain,
    There's a witness, an eye,
    Nor will charms blind that eye.

Nymph of the upland song and the sparkling leafage young,
For your merciful desire with these charms to beguile,
Forever be adored; muses yield you rich reward;
   But you fail, though you smile —
   That other does not smile.

The Ballast-Hole

Can malice live in natural forms,
As tree, or stone, or winding lane?
Beside this winding lane of ours
The fangy roots of trees contain
A pond that seems to feed the powers
Of ugly passion. Thunder-storms
No blacker look. If forth it shook
Blue snarling flashes lightning-like,
I scarce should marvel; may it strike
When I'm not by its sullen dyke!

The Recovery

From the dark mood's control
   I free this man; there's light still in the West.
The most virtuous, chaste, melodious soul
   Never was better blest.

Here medicine for the mind
   Lies in a gilded shade; this feather stirs
And my faith lives; the touch of this tree's rind, —
   And temperate sense recurs.

No longer the loud pursuit
   Of self-made clamours dulls the ear; here dwell
Twilight societies, twig, fungus, root,
   Soundless, and speaking well.

Beneath the accustomed dome
   Of this chance-planted, many-centuried tree
The snake-marked earthy multitudes are come
   To breathe their hour like me.

The leaf comes curling down,
   Another and another, gleam on gleam;
Above, celestial leafage glistens on,
   Borne by time's blue stream.

The meadow-stream will serve
   For my refreshment; that high glory yields
Imaginings that slay; the safe paths curve
   Through unexalted fields

Like these, where now no more
   My early angels walk and call and fly,
But the mouse stays his nibbling, to explore
   My eye with his bright eye.

Incident in Hyde Park, 1803

The impulses of April, the rain-gems, the rose-cloud,
The frilling of flowers in the westering love-wind!
And here through the Park come gentlemen riding,
And there through the Park come gentlemen riding,
And behind the glossy horses Newfoundland dogs follow.
Says one dog to the other, 'This park, sir, is mine, sir.'
The reply is not wanting; hoarse clashing and mouthing
Arouses the masters.
Then Colonel Montgomery, of the Life Guards, dismounts.
'Whose dog is this?' The reply is not wanting,
From Captain Macnamara, Royal Navy: 'My dog.'
'Then call your dog off, or by God he'll go sprawling.'

'If my dog goes sprawling, you must knock me down after.'
'Your name?' 'Macnamara, and yours is –' 'Montgomery.'
'And why, sir, not call your dog off?' 'Sir, I chose
Not to do so, no man has dictated to me yet,
And you, I propose, will not change that.' 'This place,
For adjusting disputes, is not proper' – and the Colonel,
Back to the saddle, continues, 'If your dog
Fights my dog, I warn you, I knock your dog down.
For the rest, you are welcome to know where to find me,
Colonel Montgomery; and you will of course
Respond with the due information.' 'Be sure of it.'

Now comes the evening, green-twinkling, clear-echoing,
And out to Chalk-Farm the Colonel, the Captain,
Each with his group of believers, have driven.
     Primrose Hill on an April evening
     Even now in a fevered London
     Sings a vesper sweet; but these
     Will try another music. Hark!
These are the pistols; let us test them; quite perfect.
Montgomery, Macnamara six paces, two faces;
Montgomery, Macnamara – both speaking together
In nitre and lead, the style is incisive,
Montgomery fallen, Macnamara half-falling,
The surgeon exploring the work of the evening –
And the Newfoundland dogs stretched at home in the firelight.

The coroner's inquest; the view of one body;
And then, pale, supported, appears at Old Bailey
James Macnamara, to whom this arraignment:
     You stand charged
     That you
     With force and arms
     Did assault Robert Montgo mery,
     With a certain pistol
     Of the value of ten shillings,
     Loaded with powder and a leaden bullet,

Which the gunpowder, feloniously exploded,
Drove into the body of Robert Montgomery,
And gave
One mortal wound;
Thus you did kill and slay
The said Robert Montgomery.

O heavy imputation! O dead that yet speaks!
O evening transparency, burst to red thunder!

Speak Macnamara. He, tremulous as a windflower,
Exactly imparts what had slaughtered the Colonel
'Insignificant the origin of the fact now before you;
Defending our dogs, we grew warm; that was nature;
That heat of itself had not led to disaster.
From defence to defiance was the leap that destroyed.
At once he would have at my deity, Honour –
"If you are offended you know where to find me!"
On one side, I saw the wide mouths of Contempt,
Mouth to mouth working, a thousand vile gunmouths;
On the other my Honour; Gentlemen of the Jury,
I am a Captain in the British Navy.'

Then said Lord Hood: 'For Captain Macnamara,
He is a gentleman and so says the Navy.'
Then said Lord Nelson: 'I have known Macnamara
Nine years, a gentleman, beloved in the Navy,
Not to be affronted by any man, true,
Yet as I stand here before God and my country,
Macnamara has never offended, and would not,
Man, woman, child.' Then a spring-tide of admirals,
Almost Neptune in person, proclaim Macnamara
Mild, amiable, cautious, as any in the Navy;
And Mr Garrow rises, to state that if need be,
To assert the even temper and peace of his client,
He would call half the Captains in the British Navy.

Now we are shut from the duel that Honour
Must fight with the Law; no eye can perceive

The fields wherein hundreds of shadowy combats
Must decide between a ghost and a living idolon –
A ghost with his army of the terrors of bloodshed,
A half-ghost with the grand fleet of names that like sunrise
Have dazzled the race with their march on the ocean.

Twenty minutes. How say you?

Not Guilty.

Then from his chair with his surgeon the Captain
Walks home to his dog, his friends' acclamations
Supplying some colour to the pale looks he had,
Less pale than Montgomery's; and Honour rides on.

In My Time

Touched with a certain silver light
In each man's retrospection,
There are important hours; some others
Seem to grow kingfisher's feathers,
Or glow like sunflowers; my affection
In the first kind finds more delight.

I would not challenge you to discover
Finally why you dwell
In this ward or that of your experience.
Men may vary without variance.
Each vase knows the note, the bell,
Which thrills it like a lover.

When I am silent, when a distance
Dims my response, forgive;
Accept that when the past has beckoned,
There is no help; all else comes second;
Agree, the way to live
Is not to dissect existence.

All the more waive common reason
If the passion when revealed
Seem of poor blood; if the silver hour
Be nothing but an uncouth, shot-torn tower,
And a column crossing a field,
Bowed men, to a dead horizon.

Biographical Notes

EDMUND BLUNDEN was born in 1896 at Yalding in Kent and educated at Christ's Hospital and Queen's College, Oxford. He was a lieutenant in the First World War and was awarded the M.C. After the war he engaged in journalism, and later went out to Tokyo as Professor of English at the University. In 1931 he became a Fellow and tutor of Merton College, Oxford. Then for a time he joined the staff of *The Times Literary Supplement*, but he once more relinquished journalism and returned to the Far East. He was Professor of Poetry at Oxford University.

In 1929 the formative experiences which, like other young poets, he had undergone in the trenches were described in a memorable prose work, *Undertones of War*. Other prose works include critical writings about Lamb, Shelley, Keats, and Hardy. He also collaborated in an edition of poems by John Clare, whose work he did much to bring to wide public notice.

Blunden's earliest poems appeared just before the First World War. They were followed by other collections, including *The Waggoner* (1920), by which his reputation was established, and by *The Shepherd* (1922), which earned him the Hawthornden Prize. Further collections have appeared at intervals throughout Blunden's life. The pastoralism of his early poetry, and its extremely English quality, at first endeared it to many readers, but told against it during the changed fashion of the 1930s. But discriminating readers have not failed to see in it qualities which lift it permanently above the common run of Georgian verse and will serve as a guarantee of survival.

RUPERT BROOKE was born in 1887 at Rugby, and educated at Rugby and King's College, Cambridge. As a young scholar of promise, he made a special study of Elizabethan and Jacobean drama, with particular reference to John Webster, and was elected a Fellow of King's in 1911. In the same year he published a small volume of poems and helped Edward Marsh and Harold Monro to plan the influential series of volumes known as *Georgian Poetry*. In 1913 he travelled across America to the Pacific, returning home shortly before the First World War. On the outbreak of war he was commissioned with the Royal Naval Division, and in the spring of 1915 he sailed to the Aegean with Churchill's ill-fated Dardanelles expedition. He died of septicaemia in April 1915 on a hospital ship, and was buried on the island of Scyros. Most of Brooke's remaining poems appeared in 1915. The definitive edition of his poetical works came out in 1946.

The 1915 volume, which contained the famous sonnet *The Soldier*, achieved enormous success, capturing as it did the mood of idealistic patriotism in which Britain had entered the war. His tragic death and the extreme physical beauty revealed by his photographs added to the legendary quality of his reputation. The legend has faded, and with it much of Brooke's reputation. Neither his idealistic vein nor the serio-comic style of the once admired *Grantchester* has much appeal for contemporary readers, and it must be admitted that whatever importance Brooke's poetry retains is largely historical. His best poems seem to be those he was writing just before the war, in which he makes a wholly serious effort to explore his own deeper feelings on a realistic plane.

WILLIAM HENRY DAVIES was born in 1871 at Newport, Monmouthshire, and was brought up by his grandfather, a publican. He may have been related to the celebrated actor, Sir Henry Irving. He was apprenticed to a picture-frame maker, but gave up and went on the roads. As a tramp in America he lost his right foot while jumping a freight train. Returning to England, he began to write of his experiences, and his work attracted the notice of established literary men. He achieved popular success with his *Autobiography of a Super-Tramp* (1907); the grant of a Civil List pension in 1911 gave him a modest independence. In 1925 he married and settled at Nailsworth in Gloucestershire, where he died in 1940.

Davies wrote a number of small volumes of brief lyrics; his *Collected Poems* (1943) contains over six hundred pieces. Not all of these are equally good, but nearly all are fresh, spontaneous, and unsophisticated. Two things inspired his best work – a simple love of common nature, and a shrewd eye for the human comedy. He is of the class of poets we call good, not great. He has not been thought worthy of a place in the *Concise Cambridge Bibliography of English Literature*, though more ephemeral writers are included; but he was a true poet, and the refusal of critics to take his work seriously indicates the limitations of modern taste.

WALTER DE LA MARE was born in 1873 at Charlton, Kent, and died in 1956. He was of Huguenot descent. On leaving St Paul's Choir School he became a clerk in the Anglo-American Oil Company. His first book, *Songs of Childhood*, appeared in 1902 under the pen name of Walter Ramal. In subsequent books he reverted to the use of his own name; it was not until he achieved some fame as an author that he was able to give up his job. In 1953 he was awarded the Order of Merit. Further collections of poems established his position as a leading poet of the Georgian period, and he was equally well known for his novels and tales of fantasy. He published a number of critical essays, as well as introductory tributes to living writers. His best known volumes of poetry are *The Listeners* (1912), *Peacock Pie* (1913), *Motley* (1918), and *The Veil* (1921). Collected editions appeared at intervals between 1906 and 1942. His anthology of poems for children, *Come Hither* (1923), achieved wide popularity.

The esteem in which his work has been held by the intelligent reading public has always been high; his reputation among professional critics has fluctuated. He was a technician of skill and a verbal melodist of subtlety and variety. The gentle, dream-like quality of much of his verse is deceptive. Reality is for him a haunted and magical area between sleep and waking, and behind it are shadows of a dangerous and sinister world with overtones of horror – a world in which de la Mare seems peculiarly at home and which he is uniquely capable of revealing.

JAMES ELROY FLECKER was born in London in 1884 and educated at Uppingham and Trinity College, Oxford. He joined the Consular Service, and in 1910 was posted to the Levant. Two or three years later his health broke down and he went to Switzerland, where in 1915 he died of tuberculosis. Beginning in 1910 he published several volumes of verse, and his *Collected Poems* were published soon after his death. He also wrote two verse plays, *Hassan* and *Don Juan*, which were produced and published posthumously. Flecker was a dedicated poet, believing, like the French Parnassiens, that a poet's purpose is not to teach anything but to aim at beauty of phrase and a timeless perfection of form.

ROBERT GRAVES was born in London in 1895, and educated at Charterhouse and St John's College, Oxford. On the outbreak of war he enlisted and was commissioned as Captain in the Royal Welch Fusiliers. In 1916 he was wounded on the Somme and reported missing. After the war he supported himself by writing, and from 1926 to 1927 he taught English at Cairo University. In 1929 he published his autobiography, *Good-bye to All That*, and went to live in Majorca, where for the most part he has lived ever since. He was Professor of poetry at Oxford from 1961 to 1966.

Apart from his poems and his autobiography, Graves has written a series of historical novels beginning with *I, Claudius* (1934), and critical works whose unorthodoxy has shocked academic circles. Among these are *The Common Asphodel* (1949) and *The Crowning Privilege* (1955). *The White Goddess* (1948), his important study of poetic myth, has had considerable influence on younger poets in England and America.

Graves is the most outstanding example of a poet who began as an orthodox Georgian and, when the movement de-

clined in the middle 1920s, transcended his earlier self and
emerged as a poet in his own right, with roots going back far
beyond contemporary fashions. He published three small
volumes of poems during the First World War, of which by
far the greater number do not appear in his collected poems.
This Georgian Graves has, with permission, been resuscitated
for the historical purposes of the present volume. Readers
may feel that, in excluding from post-Georgian collections of
his work some of the pieces here reprinted, Graves has been
unfair to himself. Of the twelve poems in this anthology, all
written before 1925, only three are retained in recent editions
of the *Collected Poems*, namely *Outlaws*, *The Haunted House*,
and *Lost Love*.

RALPH HODGSON was born in Yorkshire in 1871 and died in
America in 1962. He began publishing poems in 1907 and
was an occasional contributor to Edward Marsh's *Georgian
Poetry* and other anthologies of the time. In 1924 he went to
Japan and later took up residence in the United States.

IVOR GURNEY was born in 1890, the son of a Gloucester
tailor. He was educated at the Gloucester Choir School and
became a music student in London. In 1914 he joined the
Yeomanry, and in 1915 was transferred to the Gloucester
Regiment. He was sent to the front in 1916 and was wounded
in 1917. After his recovery in hospital at Rouen, he went on
active service once more and was gassed at Passchendaele in
August 1917. He was sent to a mental hospital in Lancashire,
where he recovered. He was discharged from the army in the
month before the Armistice. He had published a small volume
of poems in 1917, and a second appeared in 1919. He con-
tinued to develop his double creative gift of composer and
poet, and was much influenced by the Elizabethans and by
Hopkins and Edward Thomas. His mind, however, once
more gave way, and for the rest of his life he was confined to
mental hospitals in Gloucester and London. In 1937 he died
of consumption at the City of London Mental Hospital at

Dartford. A further volume of Gurney's poems, mainly from unpublished MSS., was issued in 1954, with a memoir by Edmund Blunden.

ALFRED EDWARD HOUSMAN was born in 1859 at Fockbury, Worcestershire, near the Shropshire border, and educated at Bromsgrove and St John's College, Oxford. In 1892 he was appointed Professor of Latin at London University, thus making a belated start with the distinguished academic career which followed his failure at Oxford. In 1911 he was made Professor of Latin at Cambridge, residing at Trinity College until his death in 1936.

A Shropshire Lad, published in 1896, made an immediate impression and was immensely successful. It was not until 1922 that Housman shocked the Georgian public by breaking his quarter of a century's silence with *Last Poems*. These two small volumes and his lecture on *The Name and Nature of Poetry* (1933) were the only books by Housman to appear during his life (apart from his writings on Latin authors). His *Collected Poems* appeared posthumously in 1939.

His popularity and influence were immense. Almost severely traditional – even conservative – in form, his work combines the direct expression of passionate emotion with extreme austerity and economy of diction. His irony, his stoical restraint, and his temperamental leaning towards under-statement give his lyrics a uniquely personal quality.

JOHN MASEFIELD was born in 1878 at Ledbury, Herefordshire, and educated at King's School, Warwick and on the *Conway*, a training ship for the merchant navy. As a boy he went to sea on a windjammer, but he abandoned the sea and lived for a time in New York. He returned to London and contributed to various magazines. In 1902 appeared his *Salt-Water Ballads* and in 1910 *Ballads and Poems*. The following year his reputation was further enhanced by the appearance of his first long poem, *The Everlasting Mercy*, whose coarse and slangy realism struck a new note in contemporary verse.

This was followed by *Dauber* (1913) and by *Sonnets and Poems* (1916). He also tried his hand at verse drama, and published a number of successful prose romances. After the war his long verse narrative of hunting, *Reynard the Fox* (1919), reached a very wide public. The 1923 edition of his *Collected Poems* sold over 200,000 copies. In 1930 he succeeded Bridges as Poet Laureate, and in 1935 he was awarded the Order of Merit. He died in 1967.

In the 'Georgian' period Masefield achieved a leading position among English poets, but the very qualities which had secured his popularity acted against his reputation during the reaction which followed. On the whole the anthologies, with their inevitable emphasis on short poems, have done Masefield poor service, for much of his best and most characteristic work is to be found in the longer narratives.

HAROLD MONRO was born in Brussels in 1879 and died in 1932. He was brought up in Belgium and educated at Radley and Cambridge. In 1911 he settled in London and founded *The Poetry Review* and the Poetry Bookshop in Bloomsbury, which became a discussion and publication centre for the Georgian movement. He engaged in other editorial ventures, of which the best known was his anthology, *Twentieth Century Poetry* (1929). His own verse began to appear in 1906. The *Collected Poems* were published in 1933.

WILFRED OWEN was born in 1893 at Oswestry, Shropshire, and educated at Birkenhead Institute and London University. On the outbreak of war he joined the Artists' Rifles. During the Battle of the Somme in 1917 he suffered a nervous breakdown and was invalided out. While convalescing at Craiglochart War Hospital he met Siegfried Sassoon, who showed a keen interest in his as yet unpublished poems. In *Siegfried's Journey*, Sassoon writes: 'It has been loosely assumed and stated that Wilfred modelled his war poetry on mine. My only claimable influence was that I stimulated him towards writing with compassionate and challenging realism.' In 1918 Owen was sufficiently recovered to return to France, where he was awarded the M.C. He was killed while leading his men in an attack, a week before the Armistice.

Only four of his poems were published in his lifetime. A first posthumous collection, edited by Sassoon, appeared in 1920, and a new and enlarged edition was edited by Edmund Blunden in 1931. Superficially he appears to be simply one of the realistic anti-war poets inspired by Sassoon. But Owen was not essentially a satirist. Above the horror and the indignation in his work broods a noble pity for the human condition. He sees war less as a monstrous folly than as a tragedy. Technically Owen is one of the most important and influential poets of his time; of all those who died in the war he must be considered the greatest loss in terms of unfulfilled promise. Even so, his actual achievement is astonishing. There can be few English poets whose maturity and originality were more marked than was Owen's when he died at twenty-five. He began as a romantic traditionalist with an enthusiastic admiration of Keats, and ended as an experimentalist whose discoveries in the field of assonance and half-rhyme had a seminal effect on later poetry.

The Hon. VICTORIA SACKVILLE-WEST was born at Knole, Kent in 1892 and died in 1962. Between 1914 and 1931 she published several collections of poems, of which the most celebrated, *The Land* (1926), was awarded the Hawthornden Prize. Her *Collected Poems* appeared in 1933. She has also earned a reputation in fiction, travel, and literary biography.

SIEGFRIED SASSOON was born in Kent in 1886, and died in 1967. He was educated at Marlborough and Clare College, Cambridge. On the outbreak of war he enlisted in the Royal Welch Fusiliers. He was commissioned as 2nd Lieutenant and gained the M.C. His violent opposition to the war was expressed in pacifist propaganda and in a series of bitterly satirical poems. After the war he engaged in literary journalism. His best known prose writings are the three auto-biographical studies containing the memoirs of 'George Sherston' and his war-time reminiscences, *Siegfried's Journey* (1945). From 1918 onwards he published various volumes of lyrics and satires. His *Collected Poems* appeared in 1947.

Sassoon has written lyrics in many moods, but he is at his best and most characteristic when he is either gently or savagely satirical. During the First World War he took the lead among service men who actively opposed the war. In *Siegfried's Journey* he records making notes as early as the beginning of 1916 for *The Hero* and *The One-Legged Man*, which were intended to shock public complacency and act as a counterblast to propaganda by non-combatants about glory, duty, and sacrifice. Poems of this kind were later taken for granted, and the originality of Sassoon's contribution is some-times forgotten. 'I have never been able to ascertain', he wrote, 'that my method was modelled on any other writer, though the influence of Hardy's *Satires of Circumstance* is faintly perceptible in a few of the longer poems. I merely chanced on the device of composing two or three harsh, peremptory, and colloquial stanzas with a knock-out blow in the last line.' Sassoon has also written of the influence of his junior in the Royal Welch Fusiliers, Robert Graves, who en-couraged him to write colloquially – advice which he himself passed on later to Wilfred Owen.

CHARLES SORLEY was born in 1895 at Aberdeen, the son of a Professor at the University. From 1900 the family lived in Cambridge. Sorley was educated at Marlborough, where he obtained a scholarship to University College, Oxford, but the outbreak of war prevented his going up. He joined the Suffolk Regiment, and went out to France in May 1915. In August he was made Captain, and in October 1915 he was killed in the Battle of Loos. He left a small but very promising volume of poetry, which was published in 1916.

Sir JOHN SQUIRE was born at Plymouth in 1884 and died in 1958. He was educated at Blundell's and St John's College, Cambridge. He became a journalist and was for a long time literary editor of *The New Statesman*. From 1919 to 1934 he edited *The London Mercury*, becoming the unofficial leader of the Georgians after Edward Marsh ceased editing *Georgian Poetry* in 1922. In the later phase of the movement the Georgians were accordingly sometimes referred to as 'the Squire-archy'. Squire edited a number of anthologies, of which the best known were his *Selections from Modern Poets* (First Series 1921, Second Series 1924). He also published volumes of original verse between 1909 and 1932. He was an excellent parodist.

JAMES STEPHENS was born in Dublin in 1882 and died in 1950. He was brought up in poverty and had little schooling. He drifted from clerking to journalism, and in 1911 became co-founder of *The Irish Review*. In the following year appeared his best known work, *The Crock of Gold*, a prose fantasy. From 1909 onwards his poems appeared in various small volumes, until the publication of *Collected Poems* in 1926. In his Preface he declares his faith in the lyric, which had been attacked:

A whole series of modes belong to lyrical poetry: they compose the infinity which art requires, and within which the lyrical poet may consider that there is nothing whatever which he cannot do. Lacking the feeling of power which this infinity provides, an artist is helpless. It may be said that the lyrical poet is undisputed master of all the *extremes* that can be expressed in terms of time or speed or tempo. No pen but his can hold excessive velocity or excessive slowness. A swift lyrical line is as quick as lightning; a slow one can be slower than a snail; and it is only in these difficult regions, distant regions, that the poet can work with ease and certainty.

And again:

The duty of a lyrical poet is not to express or to explain, it is to intensify life, and its essence is properly indefinable.

EDWARD THOMAS was born in London of Welsh parents in 1878, and was educated at St Paul's School and Lincoln College, Oxford. His early married life was one of struggle against poverty by means of hack journalism. He contributed critical and biographical articles on writers to various literary reviews. He began writing poems in 1912, and was encouraged by Robert Frost, who had recently come over from America to work in England, to use the unemphatic, colloquial style for which he later became known. He enlisted as a private in the First World War, although he was over the age for conscription. He had obtained an officer's commission when he was killed at Arras in 1917. His poems began to appear in 1916, and were issued in a collected edition in 1920. This was followed by several revised editions. Thomas' reputation was established slowly, and the esteem in which his work is held by discriminating readers has steadily increased. As Walter de la Mare wrote in his Foreword to Thomas's *Collected Poems*:

There is nothing precious, elaborate, brilliant, esoteric, obscure in his work. The feeling is never 'fine', the thought never curious, or the word far-fetched. Loose-woven, monotonous, unrelieved, the verse, as verse, may appear to a careless reader accustomed to the customary. It must be read slowly, as naturally as if it were talk, without much emphasis; it will then surrender himself, his beautiful world, his compassionate and suffering heart, his fine, lucid, grave, and sensitive mind.

ANDREW YOUNG was born in 1885 at Elgin, Scotland, and died in 1971. He was educated at the Royal High School, Edinburgh and Edinburgh University. In 1941 he became Vicar of Stonegate, Sussex, and in 1948 was made a Canon of Chichester Cathedral. In 1952 he was awarded the Queen's Medal for poetry. His many small volumes of verse began to appear inconspicuously in 1910 and gradually attracted the notice of discriminating readers. It was not until the publication of the first collected edition in 1936 that his poetic reputation was firmly established among a wider audience. Apart from his many short lyrics, Andrew Young wrote a number of verse plays, of which the best known is *Nicodemus* (1937). He also wrote two volumes of botanical essays. This quiet and unobtrusive perfectionist has escaped the notice of the compiler of *The Concise Cambridge Bibliography of English Literature*.

Index of First Lines

Index of First Lines

Index of Poets

Index of Poets